LIGHTNING
STRIKES

LIGHTNING STRIKES

Staying Safe
Under Stormy Skies

JEFF RENNER

THE MOUNTAINEERS BOOKS

Published by
The Mountaineers Books
1001 SW Klickitat Way, Suite 201
Seattle, WA 98134

First edition, 2002

Published simultaneously in Great Britain by Cordee, 3a DeMontfort Street, Leicester, England, LE1 7HD

Manufactured in the United States of America

Project Editor: Alisha Alderman
Editor: Heath Lynn Silberfeld
Cover and Book Designer: Kristy L. Welch
Layout Artist: Kristy L. Welch
Illustrator: Gray Mouse Graphics
All photographs by the author unless otherwise noted.

Cover photograph: *Camping in Colorado during storm* © Rex Bryngelson/
    ImageState
Frontispiece: © Photodisc

Library of Congress Cataloging-in-Publication Data
Renner, Jeff.
  Lightning strikes : staying safe under stormy skies / Jeff Renner.—
1st ed.
      p. cm.
Includes bibliographical references and index.
  ISBN 0-89886-788-6 (pbk.)
  1. Thunderstorms. 2. Severe storms. 3. Lightning. 4. Outdoor
recreation—Safety measures. I. Title.
  QC968 .R45 2001
  551.55′4—dc21

                    2001007272

Dedicated to my wife Sue, son Eric,

and my parents Russ and Gloria;

and to all my fellow meteorologists

who strive daily through their research and forecasts

to make life a little more certain and safe

CONTENTS

Acknowledgments   9
Preface   13
A Note About Safety   14

Chapter 1
WHEN LIGHTNING STRIKES   15

Chapter 2
ANCIENT GIFT, ANCIENT FEAR   25
From a Throne of Thunder   27
Lightning: Sacred Thread Uniting Heaven and Earth   35

Chapter 3
THUNDERSTORMS 101   39

Chapter 4
A ROGUE'S GALLERY OF THUNDERSTORMS   53
Mountain Thunderstorms   55
Sea Breeze Thunderstorms   56
Thunderstorms and Fronts   58
Thunderstorm Systems   62
   Squall Lines   62
   Drylines and Thunderstorms   66
   Bow Echoes   67
   Supercell Thunderstorms   68
   Postfrontal Thunderstorms   70
   Tornadoes   72
   A Glossary of Lightning   74

Chapter 5
STRATEGIES FOR THUNDERSTORM SAFETY AND SURVIVAL   75
The Four A's of Thunderstorm Safety   76
   1. Anticipate   76
   2. Assess   84
   3. Act   89
   4. Aid   92

Chapter 6

THE INVISIBLE THREAT OF THUNDERSTORM WINDS   95

   1. Anticipate   104

   2. Assess   109

   3. Act   112

   4. Aid   113

Chapter 7

THUNDERSTORMS AND FLASH FLOODS   117

The Power of Water   121

   1. Anticipate   122

   2. Assess   122

   3. Act   124

   4. Aid   124

   Hypothermia Signs and Treatment   126

Chapter 8

FROM SKY FIRE TO WILDFIRE   127

   1. Anticipate   131

   2. Assess   132

   3. Act   136

   4. Aid   137

Chapter 9

THUNDERSTORMS: THE AGELESS CHALLENGE   139

   1. Anticipate   140

   2. Assess   140

   3. Act   141

   4. Aid   141

Appendix   143

Bibliography   154

Index   156

ACKNOWLEDGMENTS

Despite bearing a single name on the cover, this book, like any book, represents a team effort. First and foremost, my thanks to the talented and patient team from Mountaineers Books that worked with me to bring this from an idea to publication. In particular, my appreciation to Margaret Foster, who first planted the seed for this book, and to Cassandra Conyers, who helped me shape and refine the idea, together with her enthusiastic support. Special thanks to my editor Heath Lynn Silberfeld, who brought imagination, creativity, and skill to the task of making this book readable and the concepts understandable, to project editor Alisha Alderman, who patiently steered this book through the whole course of production, and to Marge Mueller and Kristy Welch; their artistic talents have brought light and life to the concepts discussed. Marge in particular was faced with the difficult task of deciphering sketches from a writer singularly lacking artistic talent.

In writing a book on a topic such as this, I drew heavily upon my education, background, and daily work as an operational forecaster. I owe a heavy debt of thanks to the faculty of the University of Washington Department of Atmospheric Sciences, which granted me a degree, and particular thanks to Professor Cliff Mass. He not only helped guide my development as a meteorologist, but has also patiently reviewed this manuscript and the illustrations, correcting errors and offering suggestions for improvement. Similar suggestions and support have come from my colleague Rich Marriott. If you want to be a good at what you do, work with someone who is. We have been fortunate to share both a forecast office and friendship over the years, along with the frustrations and satisfactions of forecasting weather in the northwest.

Similar invaluable guidance came from Ed Shimon and Norvan Larson of the Duluth office of the National Weather Service; particular thanks to Ed for all the time he spent sharing his experience of forecasting the July 4, 1999 derecho in Minnesota, and for reviewing the core chapters of this book. Fire weather meteorologist Jim Prange of the Seattle office of the National Weather Service was also particularly helpful in explaining his important specialty, and in reviewing the chapter relating to it.

If this book helps you better appreciate and understand thunderstorms and their dangers together with the strategies for avoiding or evading them, it is due in no small part to the many people who generously shared their knowledge, experiences, and resources. My hometown newspapers, *The Seattle Times* and *Seattle Post-Intelligencer*, were kind to allow the use of photographs relating to the Grant-Brikoff tragedy on Mount Stuart in 1952, as well as information on the incident. Matie Daiber shared her recollections and the use of her scrapbooks relating to her husband's work in searching for the two climbers, and the successful rescue of Bob Grant. My thanks to each.

Writing the chapter describing the mythology and culture of thunderstorms drew heavily upon the knowledge of people expert in fields that I certainly am not. My appreciation to William G. Boltz, Ph.D., University of Washington, and Judith Boltz, PhD., Stanford, for information relating to Chinese history and the ancient thunder rites; to Daniel Harmon, PhD., University of Washington, for pursuing and providing relevant aspects of Greek and Roman mythology; to Donald Grayson, Ph.D., Burke Museum, University of Washington, who generously shared the greater part of a morning discussing the Pleistocene and the changes that occurred in the transition from the glacial to post glacial periods. Erin Damon of the Milwaukee Public Museum was especially helpful in providing information relating to Native American culture and faith. My thanks to the staff at that fine institution.

Jim and Lou Whittaker were generous in sharing both personal experiences and knowledge from the countless hours they've spent among and on top of the major peaks of the world. While much attention is rightfully focused on the danger of lightning strikes, Pete Esposito and Jim Brandenburg were especially helpful in highlighting the dangers of thunderstorm winds. My thanks to both for sharing their experiences and lessons drawn during the incredible July 4, 1999 derecho in northern Minnesota, as well as to Norv Larson and Ed Shimon as already mentioned. Kris Reichenbach of the Superior National Forest, Bruce Slover of the USFS, Ely and Joe Mattson of the Boy Scout High Adventure Base in the Boundary Waters were also very helpful in providing additional details.

Thunderstorms can produce rain for an incredibly long period of time, which is what makes flash flooding such a threat. However, even brief cloudbursts in the right (or wrong!) place can also result in lethal flooding. V. Reece Stein of KUTV in Salt Lake City; Tom Haraden and Cindy Purcell of the National Park Service were especially helpful in highlighting this threat. Particular thanks to Tom and Cindy for providing helpful safety guidance, photographs, and for reviewing the chapter on thunderstorms and flash floods.

For years Bob and Kathryn Harrild have offered my family friendship and hospitality at their *pension* in Leavenworth. It's only appropriate that their story of lightning-triggered wildfires help illustrate this danger. Many thanks are due the Harrilds for their recollections, photographs, and friendship. Dave Johnson and Bruce Keleman of the U.S. Forest Service were particularly helpful in providing expert information on wildfire behavior.

Countless contacts within the National Weather Service and its parent organization, the National Oceanic and Atmospheric Administration, provided help, guidance, and photographs. For that I am very grateful, as I am to my many friends and guides who have spent time with me in the mountains and on the water doing "field research"; particularly to the scouts and adult leaders of Boy Scout Troop 615 in Kirkland, which I was privileged to serve as Scoutmaster; and to my wife Sue and son Eric. In addition to sharing many hours outdoors in weather both good and bad, they endured countless hours looking at the back of my head as I worked on this book. I couldn't have written this without their support, encouragement, and understanding.

Jeff Renner
Sammamish, Washington

PREFACE

Thunderstorms, together with the dark, probably account for more sleepless nights for children (and their parents!) than the proverbial bogeyman. Everyone can recall stories offered by their parents designed to make the foundation-rattling thunder and blinding flashes of lightning a little less frightening. "It's just Rip Van Winkle snoring, dear," or "The angels are bowling up in heaven." Those and countless other variations may have helped, at least a bit, unless the child was a real worrier and began to fret "What if one of the angels drops their bowling ball?" Movies such as *The Wizard of Oz* certainly were no help, with scenes of tornadoes spawned by thunderstorms that sent houses flying, complete with bicycle or broomstick-riding witches peering in bedroom windows. "I'll get you, my pretty," they'd cackle. We were convinced they would, too. If they didn't, the thunderstorms surely would.

A little later, at about the age when dinosaurs and sharks became fascinating, thunderstorms and tornadoes were the stuff talked about on playgrounds during recess. As children became very sure of their toughness, or at least pretended they were, the stories grew wilder than the storms. "Did you hear that thunderstorm last night?" "Naw, slept right through it!" "The lightning was all over the place; I thought the whole neighborhood would go up in smoke!" "Yeah, I rode my bike up the hill to get a better look—one bolt tried to hit my handlebars, but I was too fast for it!" Keeping in mind none of those stories were true, the professed change in attitudes toward these awe-inspiring, at times deadly, yet very important storms mirrors the range of adult attitudes and behavior. Some will rush inside and into the storm cellar or basement with the appearance of a single, small, dark cloud; but there are others who will continue to climb or sail or swim or play golf with lightning dancing all about and peals of thunder so deafening some believe the end of the world is at hand. Neither is a useful response. As a meteorologist, and as someone who enjoys spending a great deal of time outdoors, I've witnessed both.

What is needed is respect and caution; attitudes born of both education and experience. That's the purpose of this book. You'll learn why, when, and where thunderstorms develop, how they usually behave, and what dangers they pose. With that knowledge as a foundation, you'll progress to gaining what might be called "street smarts" or "field knowledge"; guidance on how to use that understanding and the amazing amount of weather information available these days to anticipate such storms, and to know how to react safely. We'll examine how to assess signs in the sky and on the ground that trouble may be approaching and to learn the best actions in the face of such a threat. We'll learn that lightning is only one of four potentially deadly thunderstorm dangers. These elements are part of what I call the four As of Thunderstorm Safety. Experience may be the best teacher, but with thunderstorms, it's safer to benefit from the experience of others. You'll have the opportunity to learn both from the mistakes and experience of others in the pages that follow. Such adventures and misadventures are not only instructive, they're also fascinating—because they happened to someone else!

As a flight instructor, I used to tell students that it's always better to be on the ground wishing you were up in the sky, than in the sky wishing you were on the ground. That's essentially the purpose of this book; to help you make the best decisions so that you can safely enjoy all the beauty and wonder of the outdoors, but without finding yourself in the path of a towering thunderstorm, wishing very much that you were someplace else.

A NOTE ABOUT SAFETY

Safety is an important concern in all outdoor activities. No book can alert you to every hazard or anticipate the limitations of every reader. The descriptions of techniques and procedures in this book are intended to provide general information. This is not a complete text on thunder and lightning. Nothing substitutes for formal instruction, routine practice, and plenty of experience. When you follow any of the procedures described here, you assume responsibility for your own safety. Use this book as a general guide to further information. Under normal conditions, excursions into the backcountry require attention to traffic, road and trail conditions, weather, terrain, the capabilities of your party, and other factors. Keeping informed on current conditions and exercising common sense are the keys to a safe, enjoyable outing.

The Mountaineers Books

CHAPTER 1
WHEN LIGHTNING STRIKES

Never mistake motion for action.
Ernest Hemingway

*A life without adventure is likely to be unsatisfying, but a life in which
adventure is allowed to take whatever form it will is sure to be short.*
Bertrand Russell

Only small puffs of cumulus clouds dotted the cobalt sky on August 9,
1952, as the three climbers settled into their camp in the Cascades. The
sunset that Saturday evening set Mount Stuart aglow. There was no sense
of urgency as sometimes happens when fair weather is scarce; and fair
weather is by no means a given in the Pacific Northwest, even in August.
Autumn was still weeks away, although there were already hints of its
approach. Vine maples were beginning to glow a soft orange-red in the
avalanche chutes.

Mount Stuart, a towering 9415-foot horn of granite mantled by snow-
fields, dominates Washington's Central Cascades. Named by Captain
George McClellan in 1853 for his friend Jimmie Stuart, the peak offers
climbers stunning views of the range's east side, and of the volcanoes
Mount Rainier and Glacier Peak. Sometimes called "a mountain of thrills"
by Northwest climbers, Stuart makes a superb target for lightning. The
summit is blackened in places by past strikes.

Mount Stuart, Washington

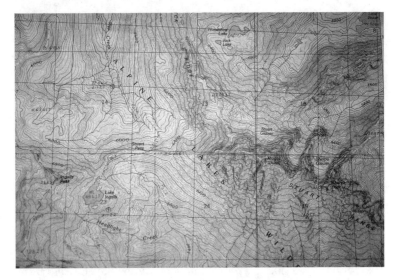

Mount Stuart topographic map, USGS

Even shortly after sunrise on Sunday, August 10, the sky didn't appear particularly threatening. Bob Grant and Paul Brikoff, both experienced climbers, set off from their camp on the North Fork of the Teanaway River. Their friend Dusty Rodes was forced to remain behind with a bad case of the flu.

Rodes probably felt some concern as he watched the small cumulus clouds begin to swell into towering dark cumulo-nimbus, perhaps just as the climbers scrambled at 9200 feet from the False Summit and over a boulder field to the summit pyramid. Grant and Brikoff had just summited and were preparing to sign the climbers' log that was housed in a small metal box. Neither of the young University of Washington students had time to hear a warning crackle of electrical charges on the summit pinnacle, to see the blue glow of St. Elmo's fire, or to feel their own hair stand on end. A surprise split-second bolt of lightning knocked both climbers to the ground, followed almost immediately by a second strike.

Grant's ordeal, later reported by several local newspapers and remembered by his rescuers, provides a chilling example of the danger posed by lightning and the need for vigilance in the outdoors, as well as graphic proof that lightning can and will strike the same place or people twice. These cautions apply as surely in the twenty-first century to those of us who live, work, and play outdoors as they did to Bob Grant and Paul Brikoff in the middle of the twentieth century. Although Grant and

Brikoff's ordeal occurred on a mountaintop, far into the wilderness, the presence of a thunderstorm doesn't require venturing beyond one's doorstep to be thrust into a survival situation.

"I crawled over to Paul. He was lying on his back. I was trying to move him. I could only move one of my legs. Then, just as I was ready to move him, the third bolt hit." Grant later remembered that as the worst of the strikes. It knocked him over a 20-foot cliff. He awoke to the agonized screams of his friend, still on the summit.

After the third bolt, Grant was paralyzed, unable to move either his arms or legs. Somehow he managed to roll off another drop-off. Grant knew he needed to get lower; he remembered seeing a sort of shelter there. Just then he heard Brikoff call, wanting Grant to pull him down. Both climbers were still attached by ropes, but Grant couldn't move. Later, Brikoff rolled over the cliff, landing near Grant.

The sky was black, the driving rain pounding off the boulders. Moments after Brikoff finally succeeded in dropping over the cliff to where Grant was lying, two more bolts struck in fast succession. Grant believed the second of those strikes, the fifth in all, scored a direct hit on Brikoff's back.

Grant had no sense of how long he'd been unconscious. The pain was intense; all he knew was that he wanted to die. "I started hitting my head against a rock. Then I thought I might have an outside chance. Paul, he wanted to die. He said he wanted to die."

Grant faded in and out of consciousness. When he finally regained consciousness, he wasn't able to move at all. Brikoff was dead.

Grant knew his position was desperate, if not hopeless; he was seriously injured, exposed, and soaking wet on the rugged peak, barely able to move and rapidly becoming hypothermic.

"All I had on above my belt was a T-shirt. I knew I

ALAN ROBERT (BOB) GRANT

VICTIM — Paul Brikoff, Seattle mountain climber, who was killed on Mount Stuart near Cle Elum, when struck by lightning Sunday afternoon.

Bob Grant, Paul Brikoff; Copyright 1952; The Seattle Daily Times *and* The Seattle Post-Intelligencer, *reprinted with permission*

couldn't survive the night with just those clothes." But Grant remembered that Brikoff had carried a sweater and spare shirt in his pack, which was still up on the summit. It was a difficult climb anytime, and even more challenging for a badly injured climber on his own.

Grant would later find out that he had third-degree burns on his back, second-degree burns on his leg, and a partially paralyzed foot. Daylight was disappearing, and the temperature was falling fast. Even if Rodes became suspicious back in camp and went for help, rescue would be hours away—and that might be too late. Now Grant wanted to live. The sheer will to survive impelled him to crawl upward over the broken boulder field.

It took Grant about 2 hours to reach the summit and Brikoff's pack. His numbed fingers finally opened it, felt for the sweater, and pulled it on. He then half slid, half rolled about 200 feet to spend the night huddled against the rocks.

"You know, it's a funny thing about shock. As I rolled down I could see the rocks coming up to hit me. But I didn't care. They didn't hurt."

It was a sleepless night, haunted by pain and the memories of his friend's death, but by daylight he was feeling better. By stomping on his paralyzed leg, he managed to hobble down the mountain. Grant arrived at the creek about 5:00 that evening. He wanted to save his left leg, which was still functioning. His right leg had no feeling.

Grant had descended several thousand feet that day to Ingalls Creek,

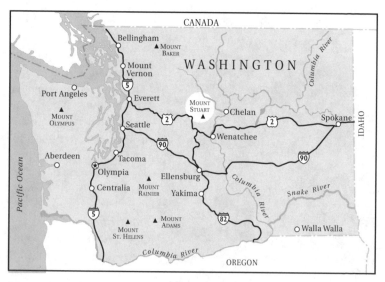

Mount Stuart's location in Washington State

hoping to find rescuers. They were on the way. Dusty Rodes had become concerned and had gone for help after Grant and Brikoff failed to return Sunday evening.

By Monday, Grant was getting worried as he felt his body stiffening, his right leg still useless. He realized that a long hike remained to the group's campsite, a hike he probably couldn't make. He built a big fire, which at least allowed him to enjoy a relatively warm night.

Bob Grant's rescue and evacuation

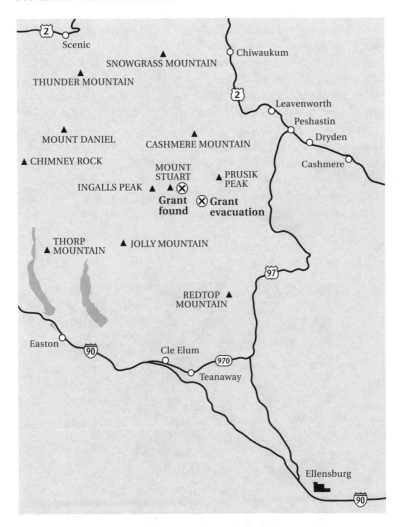

He started calling out at first light, hoping there were rescuers on the mountain, hoping they would hear him. At 5:00 A.M., the Mountain Rescue and Safety Team of the Seattle Mountaineers heard Grant's cries for help and rushed to his side.

Grant's reaction: "Human beings never looked so good!"

The search party included a physician. Dr. Otto Trott immediately administered plasma to Grant, who was suffering not only from burns but also from shock. Trott and team leader Ome Daiber had decades of climbing experience between them. They had witnessed many serious climbing accidents, but both men were stunned when they examined Grant's pack and discovered metal food cans melted and fused by the heat of the lightning strikes.

If the company and care were able to lift Grant's spirits, a Coast Guard helicopter had considerably more trouble lifting his injured body. Despite careful directions from Daiber on the ground, gusty winds and turbulence frustrated repeated evacuation attempts by the helicopter. After perhaps twenty attempted landings, pilot Lieutenant A. B. Christensen was finally able to set down in a tiny clearing surrounded by towering old-growth firs. The meadow was so small that the search and rescue team had to remove limbs from some of the trees before Christensen could attempt a takeoff with Grant. While the search and rescue team watched from the ground, the large Coast Guard helicopter

Bob Grant after his rescue; Copyright 1952; Seattle Post-Intelligencer, *reprinted with permission*

Face Reflects Pain Of Ordeal

AGONIZING EXPERIENCE—With the agony of his experience reflected in his face, Alan R. (Bob) Grant lies in tent pitched by mountaineers on meadow at 3,500-foot level of treacherous Mount Stuart while he waits for Coast Guard helicopter to take him to Seattle. Racked from illness on a washboard form a Coaster's park by rolls of historic tragic night that left him beyond and temporarily crippled from lightning bolts that killed his climbing companion, Paul Brikoff. (Story on Page 1.)

—(Post-Intelligencer Photo by Stuart Burns)

The Brikoff family awaiting recovery of their son's body; Copyright 1952; The Seattle Post-Intelligencer, *reprinted with permission.*

threaded its way up through the trees and headed toward the nearby airport at Ellensburg. Grant was transferred there to an amphibious airplane, which flew him to Seattle's Boeing Field. Grant insisted on climbing into an awaiting ambulance by himself, which then took him to Virginia Mason Hospital for treatment and recovery. And recover he did, slowly and painfully, and eventually the only discomfort Grant suffered was from his nightmarish memories. Those took much longer to fade.

The Mountain Safety and Rescue Team reached the body of Paul Brikoff the next day. Brikoff's family had come as close as they could, pacing in sorrow at the end of a lonely forest road leading to the mountain trail. Despite the team's best efforts to evacuate the body, darkness, exhaustion, and constant rockfall forced them to retreat. A second group completed that somber task later that week. They brought back Brikoff's pack. The heat from the lightning had melted the metal frame into a shapeless mess. Doctors who examined Brikoff's body estimated he was struck by seven separate lightning bolts.

It is tempting to believe this represents an isolated case. It doesn't. Every year, climbers, hikers, anglers, hunters, canoeists, kayakers, sailors, golfers, and powerboaters are injured or killed by lightning. It is true that some survivors may emerge relatively unscathed from the experience, except for a heightened respect for thunderstorms, but Paul Brikoff wasn't that lucky. It's estimated that 20 percent of people struck by lightning die. In the last fifty years, lightning has killed more than 8000 Americans. That's more than were killed by tornadoes, floods, or hurricanes, and researchers estimate the official figures may underreport lightning deaths by as much as 50 percent.

The optimist may take solace in the fact that 80 percent of those struck by lightning survive. However, many suffer long-term complications. Bob Grant's recovery was long and painful. His experience was not an exception.

SOME TYPICAL LIGHTNING INJURIES AND COMPLICATIONS

Memory Deficits	52 percent
Sleep Disturbances	44 percent
Dizziness	38 percent
Numbness	36 percent
Joint Stiffness	35 percent
Light Sensitivity	34 percent
Muscle Spasms	34 percent
Burns	32 percent
Severe Headaches	32 percent
Coordination Problems	28 percent
Hearing Loss	25 percent

Weather forecasts and warning systems weren't as good in 1952 as they are today. There were no satellites, weather radar, lightning detection systems, or National Oceanic and Atmospheric Administration (NOAA) weather radios. Could Brikoff and Grant have anticipated the potential danger by checking the forecasts? Possibly. Yet as anyone knows (particularly meteorologists), weather can be frustratingly difficult to predict and forecasts aren't perfect. Nor can weather radio broadcasts reach all wilderness areas. Were there clues warning the climbers of the impending danger? Almost certainly.

Without question, lightning is the biggest danger posed by thunderstorms. Chapter 5 explores the four As of Thunderstorm Safety; anticipate, assess, act, and aid. These guidelines are designed to be used both before you head outdoors as well as when you're there. They can't guarantee safety, but they can certainly improve your odds.

However, lightning isn't the only thunderstorm hazard. Thunderstorms can also produce flash floods, fires, and severe winds. The following excerpts are from a few true stories we'll explore in the process of sharpening our thunderstorm survival skills.

Boundary Waters Canoe Area Wilderness, Minnesota: A massive gust of wind hit, lifting the tent and Esposito off the ground. For a second, he thought the scouts might be playing a prank, but quickly realized they weren't. Goose bumps puckered his skin. It sounded like a freight train was approaching. Esposito ripped open his tent's rain fly, stood up, and looked out. It was now black as midnight, the rain pouring so hard he couldn't even see the scouts' tent a few steps away. Trees started snapping and falling. Esposito screamed, "Guys, get out of your tent!" He knew they had to get to the lakeshore, away from the trees. Before he could open his mouth again, a 60-foot pine fell, branches grazed his face, and the huge trunk fell directly on the scouts' tent.

When we think of life-threatening winds, we usually think of tornadoes. Yet thunderstorms can produce lethal winds even without tornadoes. The Boundary Waters storm is just one example. The story of this storm in Chapter 6 will illustrate how to anticipate such storms and how, if caught outdoors, to use the best techniques to avoid injury.

Zion National Park, Utah: All but two of the party had completed the last 300-foot rappel. The light mist that had started just minutes before was now a deafening deluge. It was as if a great hand had opened a faucet above the slot canyon. A waterfall plunged down the slickrock face to the left, where seconds earlier it had been dry. Purcell knew the two men on the rope had, at most, seconds to get down. Her stomach turned and her mouth went dry as she gauged the distance they had to descend. The gorge was drumming as it filled with the cloudburst. None of those below could will their eyes to move from their partners on the rope. Paralyzed by helplessness, those on the ground realized they were about to become a statistic, the victims of their own bad judgment. The waterfall swelled, blasting through the narrow chasm as if from a fire hose. The last two canyoneers disappeared from view.

Again, lightning isn't the only threat posed by thunderstorms. The volume of water released in just one minute can be enough to turn a dry streambed into a raging torrent. Each year, people are swept to their deaths by flash floods triggered by thunderstorms; still others are killed trying to save them. Chapter 7 explores how and where thunderstorms generate flash floods, how you can avoid them, and what to do if threatened by one.

Remember, too, that lightning doesn't have to strike you to be a danger. What begins as fire in the sky can set off wildfires that no human can outrun.

Chelan County, Washington: The smoke can steal your breath, and the oppressive heat your energy, but it's the sound of a fire that can immobilize you with fear. When a wildfire rips through a forest, leaping from crown to crown, the noise of combustion is louder than the biggest locomotive at full speed. Imagine the most deafening jet you've ever heard; the roar of a wildfire exceeds that. Whether triggered by lightning or carelessness, wildfires can be perversely beautiful at a distance, but terrifying up close.

These examples aren't intended to keep you indoors, but rather to help keep you safe outdoors on trail, peak, river, or lake. Thunderstorms have been around since before our ancestors walked on two legs. They're a beautiful, awe-inspiring, and indispensable part of our environment. They have shaped cultures, religions, landscapes, and languages. You can't avoid them, and you certainly can't manage them, but you can learn to act with wisdom around them.

This book places you in the shoes of people who enjoy the same activities you do but have confronted the dangers posed by thunderstorms—and survived. The chapters that follow will give you strategies to prevent an outing from becoming an adventure. The great Arctic explorer Vilhjalmur Stefansson said, "Adventures are a mark of incompetence." I offer an alternative: Adventures are a mark of inexperience and poor information. With this book, you can acquire the relevant experience from the safety of your armchair, along with sound information.

CHAPTER 2
ANCIENT GIFT, ANCIENT FEAR

(The flash of lightning, the roar of thunder; enter three witches.)
> **First Witch:** *When shall we three meet again? In thunder, lightning, or in rain?*
> **Second Witch:** *When the hurly-burly's done; when the battle's lost and won.*
> **Third Witch:** *That will be ere the set of sun!*
> *The Tragedy of Macbeth*, William Shakespeare

Nightfall had brought little relief from the oppressive heat and humidity. Sleep had come fitfully if at all; each hunter was awake but listless from too little food and water for too long. Acrid smoke from smoldering trees made it difficult to breathe.

So much had changed since their ancestors had hunted mammoths and mastodons along the margins of the great ice sheets. The glaciers had retreated, leaving vast lakes, some so large that the distant shores were invisible. It wasn't just the ice that had vanished from this land that would one day be called Wisconsin; the great elephantlike creatures these hunter-gatherers had pursued and depended upon for their existence were also

The mastodon, which lived during the Ice Age

gone. The very strategies and skills that had defined their culture were disappearing, too. Even the great carnivores the hunters had once feared were gone: the saber-toothed tiger, the dire wolf, and the short-faced bear.

At first, the warming that sent the glaciers into retreat worried no one. These Paleo-Indians, as they would later be called, still had little difficulty finding prey. Though the giant mammoths that had grazed the land and the mastodons that had browsed among stands of trees were but a memory, plenty of bison, elk, deer, and the massive stag-moose endured. Year after year, though, the climate became more extreme. The glaciers that had once stretched from the Atlantic to the Pacific tended to deflect air masses, actually moderating weather in what would eventually become the Plains and Great Lakes states. With the ice largely gone, winters became colder and summers hotter. The once infrequent thunderstorms became a greater danger than the saber-toothed tiger. Lightning strikes ignited whole stands of spruce, and entire forests went up in smoke, driving out the forest creatures as well as the hunters who pursued them.

The sun was now well above the horizon, framed by towering thunderheads. Each cloud was dimly veiled by a suffocating blanket of dust and smoke. Distant flickers of lightning suggested rain, but none had fallen in weeks. The berries and seeds the hunters relied upon when prey was elusive were shriveled and bitter. The hunting lately hadn't been merely poor; it was virtually nonexistent. The once carefully flaked stone blades lay unused, firmly bound to shafts darkened by the sweat of a thousand hunts. Why had the game disappeared? Where had it gone? Why was the land ablaze? Had they done something to displease the Great Power that gives life and takes it away? The five men had quarreled many times over whom or what to blame, but now they had no taste for argument; hunger and thirst forced the dispirited little band to their feet. The rise just a mile ahead was a moraine, glacial rubble left behind when the ice sheet retreated. The melting ice had originally left a lake on the other side. If it was still there, it promised drinking water, and possibly deer.

The faint flashes of lightning grew more distinct as they neared the moraine, but each man was too weak to notice it. Their energy reserves were dangerously low, their bodies consuming their own muscle for nourishment. A louder boom of thunder momentarily startled them, but before the sound lowered to a deep rumble, the men's dull eyes suddenly brightened. Just ahead: the lake and, resting in a scraggly stand of trees on the near shore, a small herd of deer. In a flood of adrenaline, the hunters almost forgot their exhaustion. They wanted to yell excitedly and rush headlong after this long-awaited promise of meat, but habit and instinct prevailed. The hunters fanned out silently, using every bit of cover to hide their approach.

The wind, parallel to the ridge, was blowing harder beneath the almost black sky; the deer wouldn't catch the hunters' scent, and the noise would help cover the sound of a dislodged stone. The cold, fresh air felt good. The moment would soon be right for them to burst from cover with a din. The frightened animals would flee one hunter only to run directly toward another. Success was just footsteps away. The hunters were carefully descending, all of their senses focused on the deer below, their grips tightening on their spear shafts. None felt their hair standing on end or heard the insistent buzzing that followed. Crack! The white flash and shattering explosion of thunder came simultaneously. Multiple lightning bolts sparked off the crest of the moraine and flashed forward. The shock wave knocked them off their feet.

Gradually, their vision returned, their heads pounding, their bony bodies bloodied and bruised from being hurled to the rocky slope. Three hunters rose stiffly to their feet. The deer were gone, spooked by the lightning. Where were the other two hunters? Had they pursued the deer? Searching the slope just above, they found one of their companions unconscious but breathing. Ten yards away was the other hunter, scorched and lifeless. Just as lightning long ago had given their ancestors the gift of fire, so had it taken many lives. It had now claimed yet another.

FROM A THRONE OF THUNDER

Renaissance philosophers theorized that thunder and lightning opened the minds of early humans to the idea of a divine presence, a power greater than that of any earthly creature. American scholar and mythologist Joseph Campbell suggested that thunder represented the voice of that presence, and lightning a manifestation of its strength. It was a power that could take away life but also grant gifts, such as the fire that gave warmth and light and helped set grasslands ablaze to scatter enemies or trap prey and cook food, and the rain that was the lifeblood of the land and an essential for the people.

Thunderstorms, then, are not only a dangerous physical phenomenon that is studied but still imperfectly understood by scientists; they also possess undeniable grandeur and power and provoke intense emotions. Who hasn't enjoyed watching the distant play of lightning or felt a shiver of fear as it approached? This chapter explores the roots of that emotional response and the role of thunderstorms in human history, faith, and emotion.

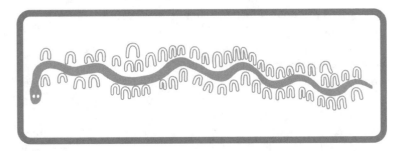

Rainbow Serpent, revered by Australian Aborigines

No written record was left by the post–ice age hunter-gatherers in the Northern Hemisphere. Only a dozen skeletons from this period have been found, but south of the equator remains a living link that extends even farther into the Pleistocene. When the continent-spanning glaciers were growing, not shrinking, the sea level was much lower. Australia, New Guinea, and Indonesia were all connected. More than 40,000 years ago, a group of humans migrated from Indonesia to Australia. We call them the Aborigines. As the oldest surviving race in the world, they provide striking illustrations of the prominence of thunderstorms in human spiritual and cultural life from prehistoric peoples forward.

The ancient religion of the Australian Aborigines is based on a creation story called "the dreaming." In the beginning, according to this story, there was a shapeless mass of nothing, eventually inhabited by what were called the "ancestors," many of which took the form of great serpents. Chief among them was the Rainbow Serpent; another was Lightning Man. Both were associated with water and life. Rainbow Serpent thrashed her tail, forming great rifts; where she lay down to sleep, great hollows formed. She gave birth to Uluru, also known as Ayers Rock, and her scales flew up into the sky, leaving an image of her colors, the rainbow that follows a thunderstorm. Thus the Aborigines see rainbows as a reminder to all of their common mother.

When they hear the thunder roll and view the livid glare, they flee them not, but rush out. They have a dance and a song appropriate to this awful occasion, which consists of the wildest and most uncouth noises and gestures.
    Watkin Tuck, 1770, member of the Captain James Cook Expedition

In culture after culture, and faith after faith, are found striking (pun intended) similarities in mythologies of thunder and lightning.

Thunder and lightning were core elements of ancient Greek religion and its greatest deity, Zeus. Revered as the father of Greek gods and humans, Zeus was often called the Cloud Gatherer. An image of Zeus is the image of energy and power. He didn't merely sit on his throne on Mount Olympus; rather, he filled it with a commanding presence. Even at rest, his eyes were charged with intent, his muscular right arm gripping a thunderbolt. In fact, the name Zeus, like that of his Roman counterpart Jupiter, is based upon a root word meaning "filled with the brightness of the luminous heavens." What could be more luminous than a thunderbolt?

It was said that Zeus's chief emblem was forged by the monstrous one-eyed Cyclops brothers on Mount Etna, a smoldering volcano. There were three brothers: Brontes (Thunder), Steropes (Lightning), and Arges (Brightness). Each was the offspring of Gaia (Mother Earth) and Uranus (Sky).

The Greek god Zeus, often called "the Cloud Gatherer"

The ancient Greeks interpreted thunderstorms as the expression of Zeus's anger, or his means of maintaining order and establishing justice. They especially believed that Zeus used his thunderbolt to punish the guilty, particularly those who had lied. Ground struck by lightning was described as "abaton": sacred and not to be stepped upon. The thunderbolt itself was referred to as "Zeus who had descended."

The Romans also considered ground struck by lightning to be sacred, believing it was charged with a potentially dangerous power. Such land was often enclosed by a wall or covered by a small temple. Jupiter was frequently described as "Jupiter Tonans"—"Jupiter the Thunderer."

Lightning and thunder have also played major symbolic roles in Judaism, Christianity, and Islam, in which they have been seen as manifestations of God and representations of God's awesome presence and power. Open a Bible to the Book of Exodus, the story of the Jews' flight from Egypt. In Chapter 19, Moses leads his frightened and dispirited people to the base of Mount Sinai to witness the presence of God, just prior to receiving the Ten Commandments:

On the morning of the third day there was thunder and lightning, with a thick cloud over the mountain, and a very loud trumpet blast.

Moses on Mount Sinai with the Ten Commandments

Everyone in the camp trembled. Then Moses led the people out of the camp to meet with God, and they stood at the foot of the mountain.
Exodus 19:16

To the ancients of the Old Testament, a thunderstorm wasn't merely a manifestation of aerial thermodynamics; it could signal divine intervention or disfavor. In Psalm 17, such a storm plays a role in the dramatic deliverance of David from Saul and other evil leaders.

And the Lord thundered from heaven, and the Highest gave his voice: hail and coals for fire. And he sent forth his arrows, and he scattered them: he multiplied lightnings and troubled them. Then the fountains of water appeared, and the foundations of the world were discovered: at thy rebuke, O Lord, at the blast of the spirit of thy wrath.
Psalms 18:13–15

Winds from a thunderstorm were central to one of Jesus' best-known miracles, the stilling of the waters at sea.

And behold, a great tempest arose in the sea, so that the boat was covered with waves, but He was asleep. And they came to Him, and awakened Him, saying; Lord, save us, we perish. And Jesus said to them; Why are you fearful, O ye of little faith? Then rising up, He commanded the winds, and the sea, and there came a great calm. But the men wondered, saying; What manner of man is this, for the winds and sea obey Him?
Matthew 8:24–27

The three disciples Jesus chose to accompany him to witness his transfiguration were James, John, and Peter, the same three he took with him to the Garden of Gethsemane before his arrest, trial, and execution. Jesus had a nickname for them: "Sons of Thunder." Some scholars say that stemmed not only from their strong witness to the faith, but also from their tendency to argue vigorously.

Into the fall of the torrent I went;
dank its maw towards me gaped.
The floods before the ogress' den
Mighty against my shoulder played.
Thirteenth-century Icelandic Sagas

The Norse god Thor, preparing to throw Mjollnir, his hammer of lightning

Centuries later, the missionary successors to the Christian "Sons of Thunder" trembled before fierce, stout-armed warriors from the north—the Vikings—who worshipped a powerful deity called Thor, the god of thunder. Son of the terrible god Odin, Thor could smash the heads of fearsome giants with his mighty hammer, Mjollnir, which symbolized lightning. Thor had to wear special iron gloves and a belt of strength to handle this hammer of lightning. Mjollnir magically returned to Thor's hand after it was thrown. He rode home to the Land of Strength in his thundering wagon drawn by two goats. The day Thursday is named after Thor. The Anglo-Saxons also worshipped a thunder-god, named Thunor, just as the early Germans worshipped one named Donner. The German word for Thursday is Donnerstag: "Thunder's Day."

For the followers of Islam; the rains of thunderstorms brought life to the desert, and their tempests punished the unworthy.

Or like a rainstorm from the sky, wherein is darkness, thunder and lightning. They thrust their fingers in their ears to keep out the stunning thunderclap for fear of death. But Allah ever encompasses the disbelievers.
    The Koran, Surat 2:19

Thunderstorms also embodied power for the peoples of the Far East, particularly in south China, which faced destructive *tai-funs* yearly. As in ancient Greece, victims struck by lightning received little or no sympathy as a hit was viewed as a sign of divine disfavor. Chinese spiritual leaders courted the forces of thunder and lightning to fight the evil spirits and phantoms blamed for misfortunes.

During the Sung dynasty (A.D. 960–1279), elaborate thunder rituals, *lei-fa,* were developed to exorcise demon spirits or destroy both the sorcerers who manipulated them and their temples. Such rituals often had colorful names, such as the "Jade Scripture of Thunderclap," and they also involved fabulous symbols, such as fire-spitting snakes or crows and wheels of fire, as described in *Religion and Society in T'ang and Sung China:*

Chinese warrior armed with later rocket version of a "fire crow"

Fire crows released in wrath set aberrant shrines ablaze; iron ropes brandished in glee entwine 'round mountain goblins.

In accounts of these thunder rituals, sticks of incense were consistently used as part of the exorcism rites, producing first a loud noise resembling a clap of thunder, then a brilliant lightning-fast flash, after which the shrine harboring evil spirits would burn to the ground. Were these just symbolic expressions in prose? A Jesuit priest, Pierre Huang, believed not. He pointed out that simply burning incense wouldn't result in a thunderous burst of flames. Huang believed it was one of the earliest recorded uses of gunpowder.

Chinese alchemists of that very period had attempted to produce an elixir of life by heating sulphur, realgar, saltpeter, and honey, an explosive combination that often burned the alchemists' "laboratories" to the ground. The first three ingredients would later prove essential to making gunpowder. Could a sorcerer have had a flash of inspiration from these mishaps and adapted this mixture to his own purposes? The power of the Chinese thunder rituals and the fear they invoked may have had less to do with the ability of sorcerers to harness thunder and lightning and more to do with the discovery of gunpowder.

Across the Pacific Ocean, more than a few North American Indian tribes used another bird to symbolize thunderstorms: the Thunderbird.

Northwest coast native version of Thunderbird

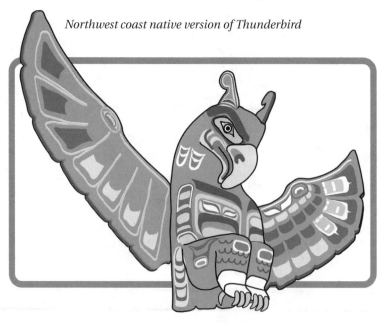

Thunderbird is a very large bird, with feathers as long as a canoe paddle. When he flaps his wings, he makes thunder and the great winds. When he opens and shuts his eyes, he makes lightning. In stormy weather, he flies through the skies, flapping his wings and opening and closing his eyes.

Thunderbird's home is a cave in the Olympic Mountains, and he wants no one to come near it. If hunters get close enough so he can smell them, he makes thunder noise, and he rolls ice out of his cave. The ice rolls down the mountainside, and when it reaches a rocky place, it breaks into many pieces. The pieces rattle as they roll farther down into the valley.

All the hunters are so afraid of Thunderbird and his noise and rolling ice that they never stay long near his home. No one ever sleeps near his cave.

From *Indian Legends of the Pacific Northwest,* as adapted by the University of Washington Department of Atmospheric Sciences for its website (www.atmos.washington.edu)

LIGHTNING: SACRED THREAD UNITING HEAVEN AND EARTH

Many stories and myths link the deities or spirits symbolized by thunder and lightning with mountains: Zeus with Mount Olympus in Greece, the gift of the Ten Commandments from God to Moses with Mount Sinai, and the transfiguration of Jesus with Mount Tabor. Such a connection isn't surprising; mountains are lofty monuments that are of Earth yet seem to stretch beyond it, distant sanctuaries where Heaven and Earth meet. Even the grandest human creations suffer by comparison. Like the tallest buildings, mountain peaks also attract lightning; if a culture believed lightning marked the presence of an important deity, what place would it revere other than a mountain?

Perhaps the most tangible (and terrifying) connection of deities, thunderstorms, and mountains existed in the Aztec and Mayan empires. Their greatest temples were the very image of the classic, pyramid-shaped volcanoes of Mexico and Central America. Aztec rulers and priests would often climb sacred peaks to offer prayers and sacrifices. Viewing rain as the nourishing lifeblood of Earth, particularly in their arid climate, the Aztecs offered the sacrificial blood of victims in exchange for that rain. The more a peak seemed to gather thunder and rain clouds, the more it was worshipped. Those sacrificed were renamed for the very mountains on which high priests actually cut out their hearts with scalpel-sharp obsidian knives.

Mayan temple at Chichen Itza, Mexico

It's not surprising that such storm-infested heights were seen by some as the lurid realm of devils, giants, and ogres. In fact, the name of the famous Eiger in Switzerland literally means "ogre." Residents of the Alps believed the rugged, windswept summits were the lair of dragons and that Satan himself lived near the summit of the Matterhorn, hurling rocks into the valleys below. Witches were thought to ride the turbulent winds around the Alps, while the much-feared Frost Giants of Viking legend were placed atop "Jotunheim," glittering mountains of ice and snow soaring above the fjords of northern Norway. The rocks themselves were considered in Norse legend to be petrified trolls: stunted, loathsome, overstuffed creatures that either ate or enslaved their human victims.

The followers of the Shinto faith of Japan also believed spirits inhabited mountains, but they perceived them as benevolent. At the end of each winter, the descent of the Yama No Kami was eagerly awaited, arriving in the form of life-renewing streams of water that transformed the dormant rice paddies below into fertile fields of sustenance. Perhaps anticipating that same process of rebirth, burial mounds or mausoleums in Japan are actually called mountains, or *yama*.

On the other side of the Sea of Japan, the Chinese considered mountains to be sacred links to heaven, embodying the principle of fertility that sustains life with water. Thunderstorms and mists weren't thought so much to gather around a peak as to actually emerge from within.

Farther west in Tibet, the Himalaya Mountains have long been sacred for Hindus and Buddhists. Mount Kailas is especially revered, though smaller than peaks better known to Westerners, such as Everest and K2. Hindus believe the divine Ganges River tumbles from heaven onto this stately peak.

Climbing a remote mountain or hill was essential to the spiritual development of Native Americans living in the Great Plains or Rockies. After ritual purification in the heat of a sweat lodge, young men were led by elders to a sacred peak or hill, left alone and exposed to the elements to pray and fast in their quest for a personal vision. The higher the peak and the more extreme the weather, the greater the potential for receiving from the Great Spirit powerful personal medicine that would define and direct their lives.

Frank Fools Crow was both a highly respected medicine man and ceremonial chief of the Teton Sioux. In the book *Fools Crow* by Thomas Mails, Fools Crow told of his vision experiences at Bear Butte, a massive pyramid of volcanic rock in the Black Hills of South Dakota.

Legendary Norwegian troll

First I heard thunder booming, and then a rich and pleasant voice said, "My friend, my friend, look up. Your friends have come to visit you." So I looked up, and from the west through swirling clouds came four riders on four running horses. The first horse was black, the second was a bright red sorrel, the third was the palomino or yellow, and the fourth was white. . . . They swept over me with booming thunder and flashing lightning following behind them, going on until they disappeared in the distance.

Fools Crow explained that the same horsemen rode from the north, then the east, and finally the south, the roar of thunder trailing behind them like the sound that follows a jet plane. As the last departed, the rich voice returned, explaining the riders represented the powers of the four directions.

The reason the riders were shown to me was to tell me I would be as strong with my medicine as they were, and that after this, their colors would be my trademark when I did my ceremonies to heal the sick.

Such symbolic legends and attitudes cross both cultures and time, providing a subconscious foundation even for our modern response to thunderstorms, and they remain a powerful theme in contemporary literature and film. In The Return of the Jedi, the third episode of the hugely popular Star Wars series, the evil Emperor Palpatine is enraged when young Luke Skywalker refuses to join his father, Darth Vader, on what is described as the dark side of the Force. The emperor fires increasingly powerful lightning bolts from his fingertips, his eyes shining with malevolent pleasure from his absolute power to destroy the young Jedi. Darth Vader is finally shaken from his allegiance to the emperor as he watches young Skywalker writhe in agony, and he finally shoves Palpatine to his death and saves his son Luke.

Trapped by a raging thunderstorm on an exposed mountain peak or a windswept lake, we know better than to believe it's an attack by a troll, devil, or giant (though our subconscious may have some doubts), but hopefully we will be stirred to prompt action. Developing an understanding of thunderstorms and using that knowledge to form strategies to ensure our safety and survival in the backcountry are the focus of the rest of this book.

CHAPTER 3
THUNDERSTORMS 101

Nature has no mercy at all. . . . Nature says "I'm going to snow. If you have on a bikini and no snowshoes, that's tough. . . . I'm going to snow anyway."
  Maya Angelou

It was a sunny, early summer day when Lou and Jim Whittaker shouldered their packs and started their climb up the Muir snowfield on Mount Rainier. The two brothers, then as now, rank for many among North America's best known mountaineers: Jim, the first American to reach the summit of Mount Everest, and Lou, the founder of internationally known Rainier Mountaineering. Temperatures were unseasonably warm that day, though the snow was still firm. The Whittakers weren't planning to summit, just to climb to Camp Muir at 10,000 feet, take a brief break, and make an exhilarating ski run back down to Paradise. Each of the brothers had a pair of metal skis attached to their packs, one ski in a pocket on each side. Skies were mostly sunny, with a few building cumulus clouds off to the east. The clouds didn't seem close at all, or particularly threatening. Lou and Jim were at 9000 feet when they heard the first rumble of thunder, followed by an odd, crackling sound. Jim turned toward Lou to ask if he'd heard the noise. Lou didn't have to answer: Electricity was arcing from one ski tip to the other, and both brothers' hair was standing on end! No sooner had they ditched their packs and run toward a hollow in the glacier than a blinding flash of lightning and booming thunder struck simultaneously, narrowly missing the Whittakers and their packs.

The Whittakers' close call was hardly a rare occurence. At any given second, about 200 lightning strikes are hitting Earth. Thus, avoiding a strike requires more than just good luck. It requires both a plan and understanding. This chapter explains the basics of how thunderstorms develop, with seemingly no evidence that a storm is brewing.

Clear skies and light winds are almost guaranteed to bring rainbow-hued hot air balloons to the Sammamish River Valley east of Seattle. Each crew first stretches out its brightly colored fabric balloon on the grassy field, then directs a fan into the balloon opening to inflate it. Only after the

Hot air balloon over the Sammamish Valley, Washington

caramel-colored wicker basket is securely tethered to the ground do the crews light the burners. The air inside the balloon warms and expands, its buoyancy gently lifting the basket as far as the tethers allow. Once the passengers and crew are safely inside, the straining ground tethers are released and the now stately balloon soars upward. The pilot fires the burner periodically to keep the air inside the balloon warmer and less dense than the air outside. As long as the air inside is warmer than the air outside, the balloon remains buoyant and keeps rising. Once the air inside the balloon cools, it stops rising and will eventually descend. In practice, the pilot can also make the balloon descend by releasing some of the air through vents in the top.

The impact of differences between balloon and air temperature on the flight of a hot air balloon

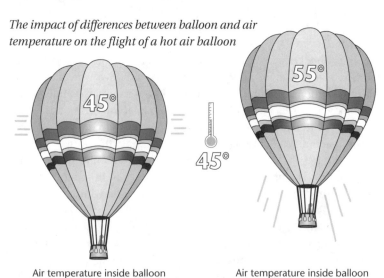

Air temperature inside balloon equals outside air temperature—balloon stops rising

Air temperature inside balloon warmer than outside air temperature—balloon keeps rising

The principle behind the operation of hot air balloons is also at work in the atmosphere, particularly in the most common type of thunderstorm found in the mountains: the *air mass thunderstorm*. Thunderstorms develop when moist air is lifted, which happens when there is a large change in temperature with height. Heating the air near the ground is one way to make that moist air rise, cooling the air higher up in the atmosphere is another. When you understand how air mass thunderstorms develop, you have the foundation for understanding the range of thunderstorm types and hazards.

If the air near the ground becomes heated enough, it will begin to rise. If an air mass thunderstorm is the atmosphere's equivalent of a hot air balloon, then the sun's heating of the ground, along with the return of some of that heat to the air above, is equivalent to opening up the burner. Open fields heat up more rapidly than forest or water, and rocky slopes heat up faster than ground covered by vegetation. We know from experience that walking barefoot on grass on a hot day is far more comfortable than walking barefoot on stone or pavement. Hot air balloon pilots know that, too; if they drift over bare pavement, they'll get a little boost upward, but if they drift over water or forest they'll likely descend. We see this process of lifting and sinking, called *convection*, whenever we heat soup

Various surfaces on the ground absorb heat and warm at different rates, which results in different rates of warming the air above those surfaces

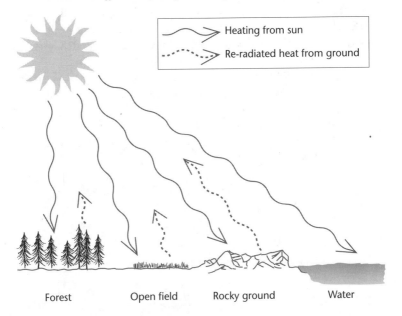

Heating from sun			
Re-radiated heat from ground			

Forest   Open field   Rocky ground   Water

in a pot. The soup over the burner heats first and rises to the top of the pot. As it spreads out toward the cooler sides, it descends toward the bottom.

Convection is the process that fuels thunderstorms, but with air and water vapor instead of broth and noodles. You may not see the water vapor, but it's there. Calling to mind an imaginary flight in a hot air balloon, if you soared high enough and the surrounding air became cool enough, you'd see your breath when you exhaled. The water vapor in your breath would cool and change into liquid water droplets, a process called *condensation.* Whenever we find that it's cold enough to see our breath, we're actually seeing water vapor condense into a small cloud of water droplets. When water vapor cools and condenses into liquid water droplets, it gives off heat; thus condensation actually adds heat to air, which helps it rise. The process is akin to opening the burner a little more in the balloon.

The transformation of the air's water vapor from a gas to a liquid doesn't always happen at the same temperature. Rather, that depends upon how much water vapor is already mixed in with the other gases that make up the air. The temperature at which water vapor will begin condensing into liquid water is called the *dew point.* If the dew point of the air is 55°F, water vapor will condense into liquid water droplets when the actual air temperature cools to 55°F. We say the air is *saturated* when it cools to the dew point.

If a lot of water vapor is mixed in with the air, the dew point will be relatively high; dew points in the 70s aren't unusual in the tropics. If the amount of water vapor in the air is a bit less, the dew point will be lower, perhaps in the 40s or 50s. This is common in the Rockies during the summer. Desert regions can have dew points in single digits, and they can be

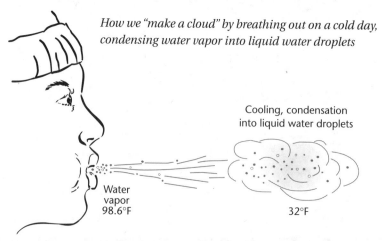

How we "make a cloud" by breathing out on a cold day, condensing water vapor into liquid water droplets

Cooling, condensation into liquid water droplets

Water vapor 98.6°F

32°F

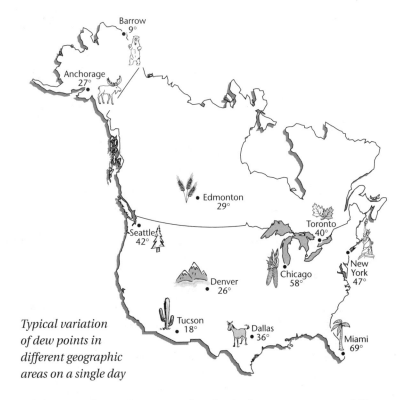

Typical variation of dew points in different geographic areas on a single day

below zero in the Arctic or Antarctic—that is, the temperature would have to cool to below zero for condensation to occur. Whatever the dew point, unless the air temperature cools to that temperature, condensation won't occur and clouds won't form. As you may suspect, warmer air has a greater capacity to hold moisture.

Relative humidity is a term commonly used on broadcast weather reports and forecasts. It's a comparison between how much water vapor the air is holding (measured by the dew point) and what it's capable of holding (measured by the actual air temperature). Relative humidity is reported as a percentage: the water vapor the air is holding as a percentage of what it is capable of holding.

If rising air does cool to the dew point, and relative humidity reaches 100 percent, the water vapor will condense into microscopic cloud droplets, thinner in diameter than a human hair. The rising air, or *thermal,* carries these miniscule cloud droplets until its temperature cools to that of the air around it and stops rising. Sometimes that happens in less than a thousand feet, and the result is called a *fair-weather cumulus:* pretty to

Relative humidity
25 percent

Relative humidity
75 percent

Relative humidity
100 percent

Relative humidity is a measure of air's changing capacity to hold moisture.

look at, but no rain. The droplets never grow large enough and heavy enough to fall through the rising updrafts of the thermal. Such cumulus clouds are fleecy with flat bottoms and gently mounded tops. Their bottoms are flat because the water vapor in the rising air begins to condense at the very elevation where the air temperature cools to its dew point. Meteorologists call this level the *lifting condensation level;* it's where water vapor in air lifted by heating or other methods will begin to condense into liquid water droplets.

However, if the rising air remains warmer than its surroundings and continues to rise, a sort of aerial game of pinball begins: The cloud droplets move up, down, and sideways in a turbulent movement of air within the growing cumulus cloud—just like the little balls in an arcade pinball game—which is why flying through such clouds can be so uncomfortable. The little droplets bounce off other droplets and occasionally stick to make bigger droplets, or fall into drier air and evaporate. The cloud begins to resemble an oversized head of cauliflower, but such growing cumulus clouds aren't made up entirely of water droplets. Because not all of the water vapor condenses right away, some is carried high enough and cools enough that it freezes. Some of the water vapor condenses first into tiny water droplets, and then it freezes. It may come as a surprise that doesn't automatically happen when the water cools to freezing, 32°F. In fact, water won't freeze on its own until it cools to roughly -40°F (40° below zero)! That may seem difficult to believe because we all have seen frost form shortly after the air temperature drops to freezing. However, when water freezes at these "warmer" temperatures, it has the assistance of grit or particles called *ice nuclei.*

Ice nuclei can be thought of as helpers in the freezing process. They can be made of dust, volcanic ash, clay, or any number of other substances. They're all around us in the air, and high up in the atmosphere, too. The more closely one of these particles mimics a real ice crystal, the faster an ice crystal will form. Sometimes a droplet wraps around such a particle like a slushball, which helps jump-start freezing. At other times ice crystals form shortly after a water droplet touches an ice nuclei. But frequently, ice crystals form when water vapor freezes directly onto a particle, without first becoming a liquid water droplet. This process is called *deposition.* Whichever process takes place, it requires both the time and opportunity for either water vapor or droplets to meet up with one of these ice nuclei. That's why you don't automatically find ice crystals in

How fair weather cumulus clouds form

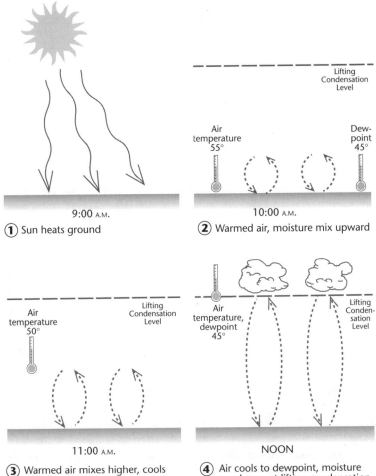

9:00 A.M.
① Sun heats ground

Lifting Condensation Level

Air temperature 55°　　Dew-point 45°

10:00 A.M.
② Warmed air, moisture mix upward

Air temperature 50°　　Lifting Condensation Level

11:00 A.M.
③ Warmed air mixes higher, cools

Air temperature, dewpoint 45°　　Lifting Condensation Level

NOON
④ Air cools to dewpoint, moisture condenses at lifting condensation level. Cumulus clouds form.

A fair weather cumulus cloud

the cloud where the air temperature is 32°F (0°C). Water droplets that exist at temperatures below freezing are called *super-cooled droplets.* Eventually ice crystals will form if the cumulus cloud keeps growing upward. As that happens, the cloud eventually meets a stable layer of air called the *tropopause,* which suppresses the rising motion. Then the powerful winds aloft will begin blowing some of the airy ice crystals ahead of the cloud, forming a distinctive flat-topped anvil form.

The pinball motion of cloud droplets and ice crystals produces bigger and bigger raindrops and snowflakes. Eventually they grow large enough to fall through or around the rising air of updrafts. However, it's not a steady process. Often a snowflake falls and melts only to get caught up in another updraft and refreeze. This process can continue several times, with frozen water droplets picking up moisture on the way up and freezing again on the way down. The result is an ice pellet or hailstone, layered with growth rings, like those found in trees. Officially, the result is called an *ice pellet* until it reaches the size of a pea, about 0.25 inch or 5 millimeters. After that it's called a *hailstone,* which can get as big as a softball. The biggest hailstone found in the United States fell in Potter, Nebraska, in 1928; it measured 17.5 inches in circumference, and weighed 1.5 pounds!

The same pinball motion that builds bigger raindrops, ice pellets, and hailstones can also create lightning. Think back to a cold, dry day. As you walked across a carpet, perhaps you scuffed your feet a little. You reached for the doorknob, but before you could even touch it—*zap!* An electric charge sparked across the gap and gave you a painful shock. Some children even make a game of scuffing their feet, trying to give each other shocks. Outside of the pain (and perhaps some fiendish delight), what's going on?

As you scuff your feet along the floor, you're separating the electrical charges. Each quarter-inch of spark that jumps from the doorknob to your finger produces a 10,000-volt difference in charge, which is what scientists call *electrical potential*. The turbulence within the cloud also helps separate electrical charges, but on a much bigger scale.

The development of cumulus and cumulonimbus clouds

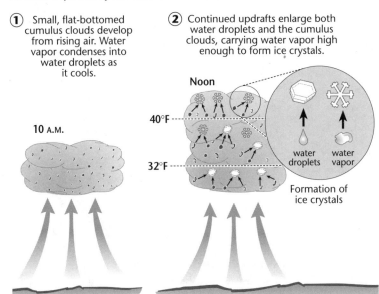

(1) Small, flat-bottomed cumulus clouds develop from rising air. Water vapor condenses into water droplets as it cools.

(2) Continued updrafts enlarge both water droplets and the cumulus clouds, carrying water vapor high enough to form ice crystals.

Noon

40°F

32°F

10 A.M.

water droplets

water vapor

Formation of ice crystals

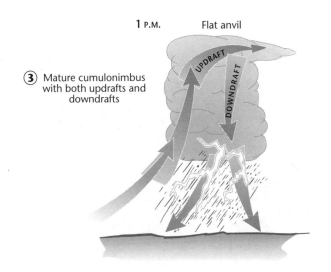

1 P.M.

Flat anvil

(3) Mature cumulonimbus with both updrafts and downdrafts

UPDRAFT

DOWNDRAFT

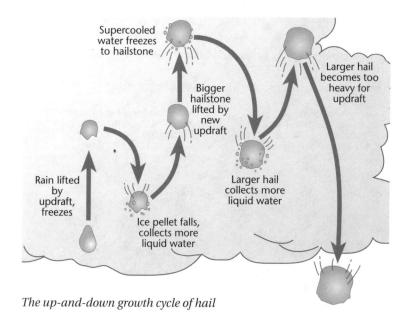

Supercooled water freezes to hailstone

Bigger hailstone lifted by new updraft

Larger hail becomes too heavy for updraft

Rain lifted by updraft, freezes

Ice pellet falls, collects more liquid water

Larger hail collects more liquid water

The up-and-down growth cycle of hail

The updrafts and downdrafts within a building thunderstorm vary in speed, from a few feet per second to as much as 100 miles per hour. The vast scale of the pinball game within the cloud sorts out different-size particles that carry different electrical charges. The heavier particles carry a negative charge toward the base of the cloud, while the updrafts lift the smaller, lighter particles with positive charges to the upper part of the cloud. That's how one popular theory explains why much of the upper part of the thunderstorm becomes positively charged, and much of the lower part negatively charged. The surface of Earth also tends to be negatively charged.

Hail on the ground after a typical thunderstorm (photo courtesy of NOAA)

Because like charges repel (think of trying to put the negative ends of two magnets together), the negative charges near the cloud base push away the negative charges on the ground, leaving a positive charge. Some of that positive charge flows up large objects, such as mountain peaks, towers, even people. That's why your hair can stand on end if you're close to a thunderstorm. Those positive charges are blocked from continuing to flow up into the thunderstorm because the air tends to hinder, not help, the flow of electricity. That tendency is called *resistance.*

Consider the buildup of negative charges within the lower part of the cloud to be like water building up behind a dam. As the pressure builds (in this case the electrical potential, or voltage), eventually the dam (the natural resistance of the air) can't hold back all the negative charges, and some flow toward the ground. They don't move in one vast flood; if they did it would eclipse any special effect ever conceived in Hollywood.

The negative charges move haltingly downward in what's called a *stepped leader,* typically about as thick as a pencil. As this stepped leader approaches the ground, it attracts the positive charges, which typically move up something tall like a tree or rocky pinnacle in what's called a *streamer.* As they connect, a flood of positive charges surges back up to the cloud at about one-third the speed of light, in the much bigger and brighter return stroke. That's the actual lightning bolt we see. This immense flow of electricity superheats the surrounding air to as much as 50,000°F, far hotter than the surface of the sun! This heating sets off a shockwave that exceeds the speed of sound. The resulting sonic boom is what we call thunder.

Once the stepped leader and streamer connect, several pulses of electricity can surge through the channel, producing repeated flashes. A single lightning bolt doesn't flicker; that comes from repeated flows in the same channel. Because the near-speed-of-light movement of lightning is much faster than the speed of sound, we see the lightning first and then hear the thunder. That difference can be used to estimate the distance of the thunderstorm. (See Chapter 5.)

The life cycle of one of these air mass thunderstorms is typically less than an hour. Lightning can be a danger during the *developing stage* as the cloud builds upward. There's very little rain then; almost microscopic cloud droplets are being carried upward, colliding, and enlarging, and ice crystals are beginning to form. Lightning is a major hazard during the *mature stage,* marked by updrafts and downdrafts within the cloud. This stage produces heavy rain, hail, winds, and lightning. However, even after the downdrafts choke out the updrafts and the storm enters the

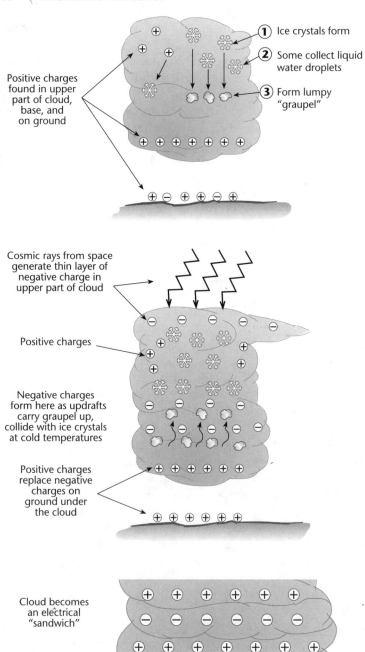

How electrical charges separate in a growing cumulus cloud

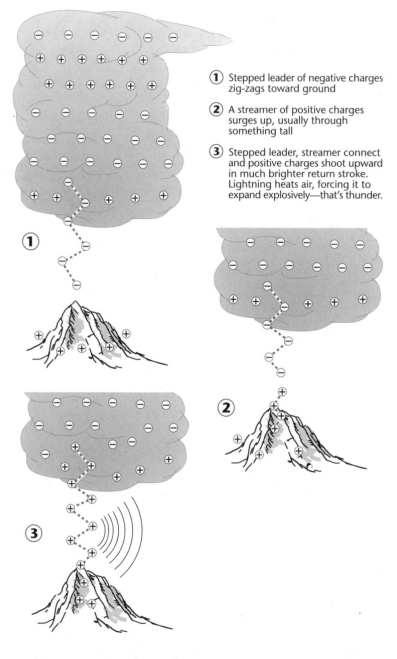

1. Stepped leader of negative charges zig-zags toward ground

2. A streamer of positive charges surges up, usually through something tall

3. Stepped leader, streamer connect and positive charges shoot upward in much brighter return stroke. Lightning heats air, forcing it to expand explosively—that's thunder.

How lightning and thunder develop

dissipating stage and begins to die, lightning remains a danger. What, you say, of the old story about a bolt out of nowhere? It's true. Lightning can strike objects up to 10 miles from the side of a massive thunderhead.

Although these air mass thunderstorms typically last only 30 to 50 minutes, other thunderstorms do last much longer and move much farther. We'll explore those in the next chapter, "A Rogue's Gallery of Thunderstorms."

CHAPTER 4
A ROGUE'S GALLERY OF THUNDERSTORMS

The magic of the craft has opened for me a world in which I shall confront, within two hours, the black dragons and the crowned crests of a coma of blue lightnings, and when night has fallen I, delivered, shall read my course in the stars.

Wind, Sand and Stars, Antoine de Saint-Exupéry

The flight from Madison back to Milwaukee's Mitchell Field had been quiet. The weather briefing earlier in the day had shown a stationary front draped between the two Wisconsin cities, but with little activity. Though I'd spent much of the flight out and virtually all of it back enveloped in clouds, only the last few minutes had brought more than a light sprinkle. Rain was now hissing on the windshield, rising occasionally into a crescendo. A quick glance at the outside air temperature gauge confirmed it was still too warm to be concerned about ice glazing over the wings. That was as it was supposed to be—small, single-engine aircraft don't fly well when they're transformed into snowballs with wings. The engine instruments were reassuring; all the horses under the hood were galloping smoothly, and although I couldn't see beyond the propeller, the navigation instruments showed I was on course. If there were no traffic delays in getting vectored for the final approach, I'd be on the ground in less than 20 minutes.

The monotonous hissing of rain shifted into the cascade of a waterfall. I seemed no longer to be flying through a cloud, but through an ocean. A sudden jerk, and I was weightless; a giant hand seemed to be pushing my little plane toward the ground. The vibrating instruments were difficult, almost impossible, to read as the airplane shuddered during its sudden descent. Hard as I tried, I couldn't reach the throttle to reduce power. When I tried to move my right hand the 12 inches from control wheel to throttle, it seemed to sway drunkenly ahead and to the left. With great concentration, I moved my hand back to the left; now the throttle lurched to the right. I had to reach it. Maintaining my present airspeed, paired with the abrupt shudders and shakes, could overstress the small Beechcraft. Slowing my airspeed would prevent the downdraft from bending my wings, and at the moment, I was descending very fast.

The control wheel came alive in my left hand, threatening to slither out of my grasp. I grabbed it with both hands, just as the plane shuddered with another jolt, and then began to shake violently. The instruments were nothing but round blurs on the black panel in front of me. The shaking stopped and suddenly I was rising—fast. My mouth tasted worse than old dishwater and I ached all over. My legs began to shake like a sewing machine as I tried to keep my feet on the rudder pedals. The plane couldn't take much more of this. I made a fast grab for the throttle and finally reached it. There, with power reduced, I expected my wings to stay on. I abruptly let out an involuntary sigh of relief, but then the hammering of rain was joined by a slow rumble: thunder. It seemed to fill the airplane. I felt myself vibrating with the force. Either my head was growing or my eyes were shrinking. My head ached. There was a sudden blast of light. For a second I was convinced I had been hit by lightning. But the shaking and hammering stopped. The white in front of my eyes resolved to blue. I realized I was out of the cloud, and then I was blinded by the sudden exposure to sunlight. My vision returned. I looked suspiciously at the now quiet instruments and saw I was left of course. My hands trembled a bit as I corrected to the right. Next, I quickly glanced at the wings. All the parts seemed at least to be flying in formation if not firmly attached to each other. My neck, shoulders, back, and arms all ached as I turned to look behind me. The cloud I just flew through seemed to be boiling upward and outward. I glanced at the low deck of clouds just below, trying to forget the thunderstorm behind and to focus on the task of getting the plane back on the ground. Just two thoughts hovered in the back of my mind: I never want to do that again, and I want to find the men's room.

The air mass thunderstorms discussed in the previous chapter have a fairly predictable pattern: Puffy cumulus develop in the morning, swell into towering cumulo-nimbus during the afternoon, then dissipate as the sun sets. That's why climbers often say "Move high in the morning, go low in the afternoon." That's a good general principle. Such clouds are relatively easy to see, but anyone who's spent much time outdoors knows that many thunderstorms don't follow that pattern. The thunderstorm I flew through was just one example. No thunderstorm is to be taken lightly, whether you're in the air, on the water, or firmly on the ground.

Understanding the different types of thunderstorms will help anyone to better understand potential dangers and to develop some strategies to either stay safe or get safe. You may only have one chance to make the correct choice. That's the focus of the next two chapters: to examine the virtual rogue's gallery of thunder and lightning storms, and then to use that basic knowledge to develop some strategies for survival.

MOUNTAIN THUNDERSTORMS

Spend much time in the mountains and you'll become firmly convinced the peaks and ridges can generate their own weather. It's true. The higher the peak, the more sparse the vegetation. Less vegetation means more exposed soil and rock. As mentioned earlier, rock and gravelly soil heat up much more rapidly than ground covered with trees and plants. That heating develops thermals, which carry moisture upward and jump-start thunderstorms faster than would happen over less rugged and barren terrain.

So, the tendency is for such thunderstorms to develop during the afternoon hours, and thunderstorms develop when moist air rises. That boost can come from heating near the surface or cooling aloft, and the boost from heating is greatest during the afternoon hours. That certainly happens in the mountains, but that source of lifting can be amplified or replaced by another source: winds flowing against, up, and over either an isolated peak or an entire ridge. Along with the upslope flow already discussed, this is what's called an *orographic effect*.

When such prevailing winds move against a mountain peak or ridge, they boost the natural tendency of thermals to carry moist air aloft, and they can set off the convection that triggers thunderstorms. This influence also allows such thunderstorms to persist much longer, occasionally into well after dark. The downslope winds on the leeward side of the peak or ridge will tend to suppress thunderstorms. This might suggest that if you know the general direction of winds aloft, you can better anticipate on which side of a mountain ridge thunderstorms will tend to develop, but it's important to recognize that doesn't mean you'll be safe from thunderstorms along the lee or downwind side of a peak or ridge. Winds aloft can shift the thunderstorms that develop farther downwind. Planning your climb or hike for the leeward side of a ridge may improve your margin of safety, but you'd better keep an eye out for evidence of thunderstorms drifting downwind. (See Chapter 6 for more information about such winds, whether you're at home or in the field.)

Winds moving around a peak or ridge can also converge on the downwind side. As those winds converge, the moist air often has no direction to go other than up, which can set off thunder showers. Such showers typically are not directly over the leeside slopes, but at a distance downwind.

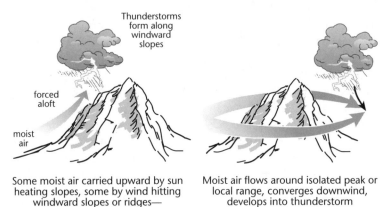

Thunderstorms form along windward slopes

forced aloft

moist air

Some moist air carried upward by sun heating slopes, some by wind hitting windward slopes or ridges—develops into thunderstorm

Moist air flows around isolated peak or local range, converges downwind, develops into thunderstorm

How mountains influence where thunderstorms develop

To summarize:

► Mountain thunderstorms are most frequent during the afternoon.
► Mountain thunderstorms are most frequent along the windward slopes, especially if cooler air has moved in aloft and sun is warming the slopes.
► Mountain thunderstorms may form downwind of smaller ranges or isolated peaks in a convergence zone.

SEA BREEZE THUNDERSTORMS

The sea breeze is another consequence of different substances heating up at different rates. Because land heats up more rapidly than water, as the inland air rises, the ocean air tends to flow inland during the day. Such sea breezes typically develop during the late morning and early afternoon hours, though the exact timing can vary from place to place. Sea breezes, despite their name, aren't confined to ocean coasts; they can also occur along inlets or even larger lakes. As cooler ocean or lake air moves inland, the boundary between that air and the warmer air inland effectively forms a *front*, which is simply a boundary between two different air masses. (An *air mass* is simply a body of air that's fairly uniform in temperature and moisture.) Such a sea breeze front commonly triggers thunder showers along the Atlantic and Gulf Coast regions of the United States.

This same effect can be amplified along peninsulas such as Florida or the Baja peninsula of Mexico. Sea breeze fronts move inland from either side of the peninsula, converge over land, and set off some impressive atmospheric fireworks.

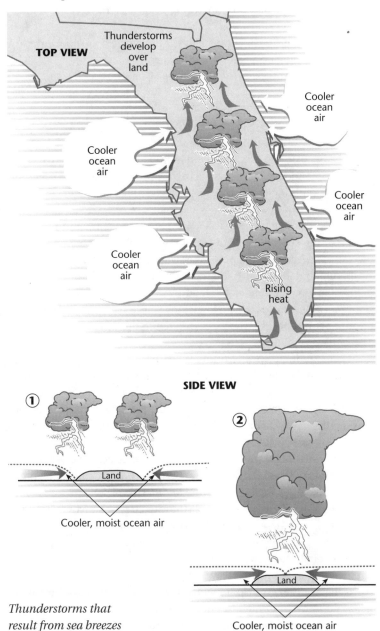

Thunderstorms that
result from sea breezes

- ► Sea breezes are strongest when other weather systems are absent.
- ► Disturbances producing significant winds or clouds can prevent sea breezes from developing.
- ► Sea breezes typically develop during the late morning hours and peak during the afternoon.
- ► Sea breeze thunderstorms usually die out as the flow reverses late in the day, moving from land toward water.
- ► Particularly strong sea breeze thunderstorms are found over peninsulas.

THUNDERSTORMS AND FRONTS

In summary, thunderstorms need moisture, something to lift that moisture, and air that cools enough with altitude so the moisture can keep rising. That tendency (as discussed in the previous chapter) is called *instability,* a condition that usually exists when much cooler air lies on top of warmer air. That's what helps hot air balloons rise.

In air mass thunderstorms, either the heating of moist air near the ground or the cooling of air higher up provides that initial boost. *Orographic thunderstorms* happen either with the heating of moist air near the ground that then rises as thermals develop along hills or mountains, or with the forced lifting of moist air by wind moving against and up a mountain. Still another way to force moist air to rise enough to produce a thunderstorm occurs when two different types of air masses collide, such as along a front.

There are four types of fronts. A *warm front* is a boundary where warm air is replacing colder air. A *cold front* is a boundary where cold air is replacing warmer air. A *stationary front* is a boundary between warm and cold air that isn't moving much at all. An *occluded front* combines the qualities of warm and cold fronts and forces warm air up when two colder air masses collide.

The formation or presence of low pressure makes air masses move to create fronts. Watch any television weather forecast, and you'll probably hear the terms *high pressure* and *low pressure.* High pressure is simply a zone of sinking air; as it piles up, the pressure rises, just as the weight on a scale would increase if you kept piling on the pounds. The barometer that meteorologists use to measure air pressure is nothing more than a scale that measures the weight of the air above. Low pressure is an area where air is rising up and away. The pressure decreases, or gets lower, just as the reading on a scale would if you shed some pounds. Ordinarily, air would move from high to low pressure just as it would flow from a balloon if you were to stop pinching the neck.

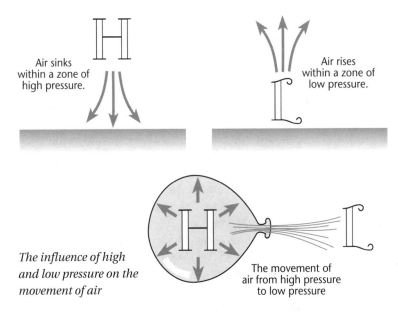

Air sinks within a zone of high pressure.

Air rises within a zone of low pressure.

The influence of high and low pressure on the movement of air

The movement of air from high pressure to low pressure

However, the earth rotates and that makes the movement of air more complicated. Not only does air sink in an area of high pressure, but it also spreads out and rotates clockwise around the center of that high in the northern hemisphere. As the air rises up and out from an area of low pressure, it rotates counterclockwise. (The opposite is true south of the equator, but for the purposes of this book, let's stick with the northern hemisphere.)

That behavior typically brings warmer air from the south toward the north ahead of a low, or behind a high; and it usually brings cooler air from the north toward the south behind a low, or ahead of a high. That's why air masses move and collide and form fronts.

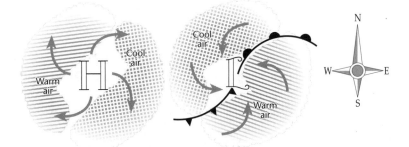

The circulation of air around highs and lows that results from the rotation of Earth, and how that generates warm and cold air masses

Fronts don't exist only at the surface of Earth; they also extend up into the atmosphere. When cool air meets warmer air, the warmer air rises because it is less dense and lighter. That warm air carries the moisture needed to create clouds and rain and sometimes thunderstorms.

Notice that along a warm front, the warm air gradually slides up and over the cold air it's replacing. This is a stable situation, and one that rarely leads to the rapid and sustained lifting that's needed to produce a thunderstorm. That's why flat, *stratus* clouds with widespread precipitation are typically found along and, especially, ahead of a warm front. There can be areas of more intense precipitation, referred to as *rain bands,* and occasionally under special circumstances even a thunderstorm. However, a warm front is not a particularly common place to find thunderstorms. Once the warm front moves through, though, thunderstorms and possibly severe thunderstorms are a distinct possibility.

A cold front behaves like a snowplow; it rapidly boosts upward the warmer and often moist air ahead of it. This kind of lifting can easily produce thunderstorms and often does, and it is why towering cumulus clouds are typically found along a cold front.

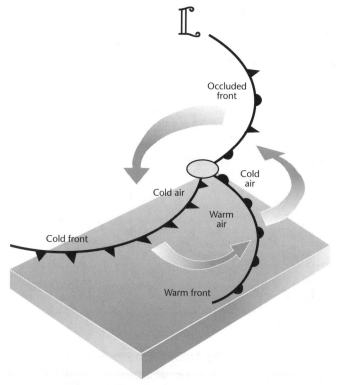

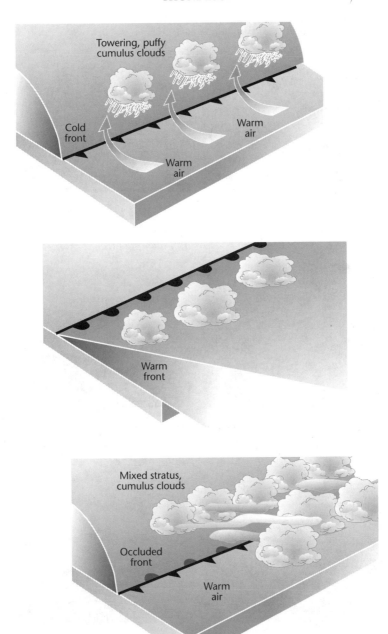

How air moves along different fronts and air masses, resulting in different types of clouds

Cloud Identification Chart

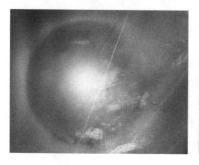

Halo, commonly seen 24–48 hours ahead of precipitation

Lenticular cloud, wavelike clouds over mountains often suggesting approaching precipitation

Cirrus clouds, high clouds often seen before the arrival of a warm front

Cirrostratus clouds, high clouds often seen before the arrival of a warm front

Altostratus clouds, mid-level clouds often seen after cirrus clouds and before the lower stratus clouds when a warm front is approaching

Stratus clouds, flat, layered clouds often seen with the approach of a warm front and precipitation, or the arrival of ocean air

Nimbostratus, stratus clouds producing widespread precipitation and often lowered visibility

Altocumulus, mid-level cumulus clouds marking unstable air that often indicate the potential for thunder or rain showers later in the day

Cumulus, lower clouds that mark unstable air. With continued growth, these often indicate the potential for thunder or rain showers later in the day

Cumulonimbus, cumulus clouds producing rain, snow or thunder, lightning and hail

Stratocumulus, lumpy, layered clouds that can produce showers

An occluded front typically occurs when cold air pushes through warmer air, running into another cold air mass. Sometimes it shoves under the cold air ahead, and sometimes it pushes over it, depending upon which of those two air masses are colder. Because warm air is abruptly forced upward, occluded fronts are another common place for thunder shower formation.

Stationary fronts occur when the boundary between the cold and warm air masses isn't moving. Typically this produces widespread clouds. Occasionally this can also produce thunderstorms.

When you learn of a forecast that tells you a front is approaching the area of your planned outing, it's time to ask two important questions: Are thunder showers forecast? How exposed would I be to thunder showers given the location and type of activity planned? (See the following chapter for more important information about these questions.) In any case, always remember the following:

► Thunderstorms occasionally form along warm fronts and stationary fronts.
► Thunderstorms frequently form along cold or occluded fronts.
► Thunderstorms frequently form in the warm air between warm and cold fronts.

Some of the worst thunderstorms develop between cold and warm fronts.

THUNDERSTORM SYSTEMS

Meteorologists call some of the worst entities in the thunderstorm world *MCS's (mesoscale convective systems)*. That's a fancy way of saying they're a system of thunderstorms ranging in size from roughly twelve to several hundred miles. An MCS can evolve from just one thunderstorm cell or a group of them. They can last 3 hours or more—much longer than air mass thunderstorms—and they come in a variety of shapes and sizes.

Squall Lines

Squall lines may begin life as a line of thunderstorms or as a loose cluster of thunderstorms. If a squall line moves over your camp, it's an experience you won't soon forget. Heavy rain, high winds, hail, intense lightning, and even tornadoes can come out of this seemingly endless wall of thunderstorms. Like any thunderstorm, a squall line needs a few specific ingredients: moist air near the surface; cooler, drier air above; and a change in wind speed or direction with altitude.

Warm, moist air flowing into the squall as it surges forward supplies the lifeblood of the storm. As the clouds swell upward, the wind shear, or change in wind speed or direction, prevents the descending cold air from choking off the supply of warm, moist air. That's why squall lines last much longer than most individual thunderstorms. Occasionally, the descending pool of cold air, as it hits the ground and spreads out, may trigger a new squall line as it forces moist air upward ahead of the old squall line. It's also common to find a line of flat stratus clouds to the rear of the squall line, producing widespread but lighter rainfall.

Although the rainfall, lightning, and hail may decrease after the squall line passes, it's not time to let your guard down. While the strongest winds typically occur beneath or ahead of the line, occasionally severe winds are found behind. The descending cold air forms a zone of higher pressure, and the air forced up to form the stratus clouds to the rear forms a zone of lower pressure. If the difference in pressure is great enough, strong winds may develop as the cold air accelerates toward the lower pressure to the rear.

This seemingly endless line of thunderstorms can either lumber forward or sprint across one county after another, depending upon the winds at higher altitudes. Less powerful squall lines have a life cycle of 3 to 5 hours, while the strongest may persist 12 hours or more. Once the squall line passes, it's wise to allow at least a half hour before you venture out, but that's hardly a guarantee of dry weather. The stratus clouds that form to the rear of a squall can produce widespread rain for hours.

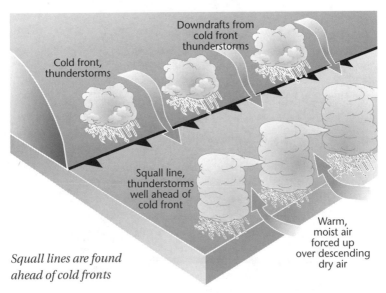

Downdrafts from cold front thunderstorms

Cold front, thunderstorms

Squall line, thunderstorms well ahead of cold front

Warm, moist air forced up over descending dry air

Squall lines are found ahead of cold fronts

Following are a few key points about squall lines:

► Squall lines typically form along or ahead of a cold front.
► One squall line can cause formation of another squall line ahead of it.
► Expect strong gusty winds, hail, lightning, and possibly tornadoes.
► Widespread rain is likely even after a squall line dies or moves past.
► Strong winds can occur after a squall line moves past.
► Allow at least a half hour after squall line passage before venturing out.

In the Rocky Mountains, thunderstorms that first develop over the peaks and ridges can trigger squall lines to the east that move from the Front Range toward the Great Plains. As these thunderstorms mature and begin to dissipate over the Rockies, the cold air within the storms rushes toward the surface, through the canyons, and toward the plains. This outflow of cold air from the canyons can lift the warmer, moist air to the east, giving birth to new thunderstorms. Occasionally, such outflows can merge, producing an eastward-moving squall line.

Drylines and Thunderstorms

Just as the colder, drier air emerging from the canyons of the Rockies can trigger thunderstorms to the east in the central and northern Plains states, another phenomenon farther south called the *dryline* is capable of setting off strong thunderstorms, and even tornadoes.

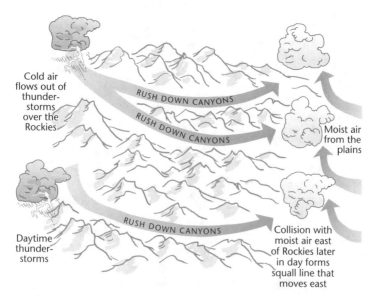

Cold air flows out of thunderstorms over the Rockies

RUSH DOWN CANYONS

RUSH DOWN CANYONS

Moist air from the plains

RUSH DOWN CANYONS

Daytime thunderstorms

Collision with moist air east of Rockies later in day forms squall line that moves east

How thunderstorms over the Rockies can produce squall lines

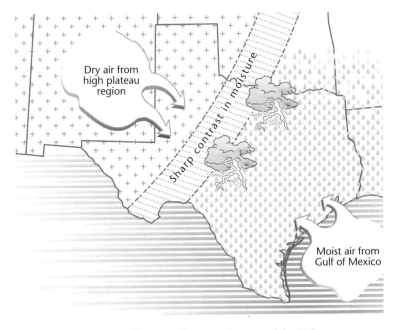

The formation of a dryline over the central states of the U.S.

The dryline is simply a narrow zone of sharp changes in moisture; it forms when dry air flowing off the arid high plateau regions of Mexico and the Southwestern states meets moist air from the Gulf of Mexico to the east. Although they can occur anytime, drylines are most common during the late spring and early summer months and can persist for days. Although drylines have been found as far north as Nebraska and the Dakotas, they're usually seen in western Kansas and the Oklahoma and Texas panhandles. The thunderstorms that develop typically become well organized in lines of moderate to strong intensity. If you hear forecasters mention drylines and thunderstorms in the same breath, keep the following in mind:

► Thunderstorms tend to drift east during the day.
► Thunderstorms tend to move fastest to the east during the morning.
► Thunderstorms tend to drift west at night.
► Thunderstorms tend to move fastest to the west before midnight.

Bow Echoes
Bow echoes are curved lines of thunderstorm cells that may begin either as a line of thunderstorms or a single isolated cell. The name comes from the shape that appears on radar screens. These storms aren't notable

because of their size; bow echoes typically range from 10 to 70 miles long. As they begin to curve into their characteristic bow shape, though, dry air several miles above the ground can be drawn into the storm. The colder, heavier air plunges earthward, carrying the momentum of the faster winds aloft. The resulting hurricane-force winds can cause enormous damage on the ground. When at least three different observations of hurricane-force winds separated by 40 miles or more have been made and those winds sweep a path of at least 250 miles, these destructive storms are called *derechos* (day-ray-choes) from the Spanish word for "straight ahead." We'll explore this form of meteorological mayhem in greater detail in Chapter 6.

Supercell Thunderstorms

If derechos have the destructive power of a strike fighter, then *supercells* are equivalent to an entire bomber squadron. Supercells can cover whole states and as much as 100,000 square miles of land. The greater the change in wind speed and direction with altitude, the greater the potential for violent weather.

Supercells belong to the MCC (mesoscale convective complex) class of thunderstorm. They're related to the other thunderstorm systems already discussed; they're just bigger, more violent, and longer lived. Thunderstorms by their very nature are suicidal; the powerful downdrafts that can produce widespread damage also kill them off. But MCCs not only rotate vertically, they also generate a rotating, horizontal tube of storm air. That prevents downdrafts from choking out the updrafts of warm, moisture-laden air. That power and longevity are why these mesocyclones can spawn a series of large, long-lived tornadoes capable of obliterating entire towns or forests. Look at a satellite image of a supercell; if anything is surprising, it's that anything in its path could survive.

If the rotation is so important to these superstorms, where does it come from? In two words, *wind shear,* a change in wind speed and direction with altitude. This creates a rolling tube of air. That spinning tube may be tilted or lifted by rising air near the surface, like a Slinky toy lifted in the middle. Once it begins to spin standing on one end, it's the beginning of a mesocyclone.

As the cold, dry air aloft plunges to the ground, it spreads out in a *gust front,* a forward-moving pool of cool air that generates gusty winds; this acts as a plow, driving more warm, moist air into the mesocyclone to keep it going. The tilt of the storm prevents the descending cold air from drowning out the updrafts. Initially, a mesocyclone may be about 10 to 12 miles wide and perhaps 40,000 feet high. The most intense rainfall

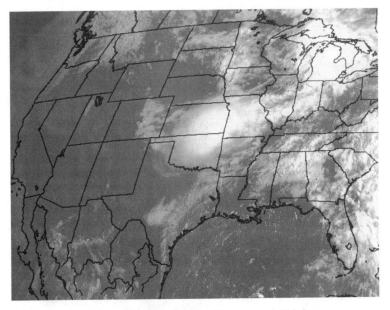

Satellite image of a supercell storm over Kansas and Oklahoma (photo courtesy of NOAA)

will be in the middle, as viewed from above. As it begins to mature, it will develop a teardrop shape, with the heaviest rain near the southwest corner. At this point, the storm continues to expand, swelling up to 50,000 feet. The "adult" form of one of these mesocyclones will swell even higher, perhaps as much as 60,000 feet—that's 12 miles high—and will resemble a crooked teardrop; tornadoes are often found on the edge of the crooked part, what's often called a "hook echo" on radar. As this "wraparound" process continues, the southern part of the storm may block the supply of warm, moist air from reaching the northern part, and it will begin to die. As long as the storm continues to rotate, however, it can develop again and again.

To summarize:

- ► Mesocyclones produce frequent lightning, heavy rain, strong winds, and—occasionally—tornadoes.
- ► Mesocyclone rainfall is capable of producing flash flooding.
- ► Any possibility of a mesocyclone is reason to stay at home or get home immediately.
- ► Seek shelter immediately from any thunderstorm that seems to stretch from horizon to horizon.
- ► If the lower part of a cloud is rotating, assume it may produce a tornado at any time.

The making of a mmesocyclone and a supercell storm

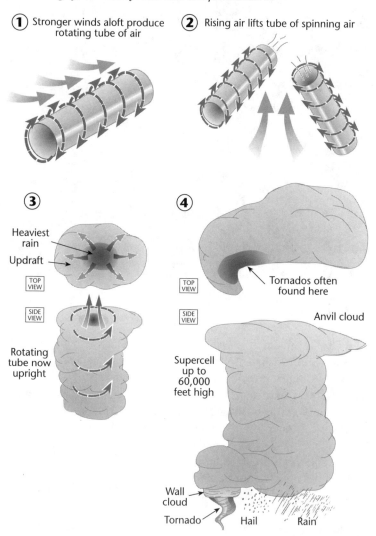

① Stronger winds aloft produce rotating tube of air

② Rising air lifts tube of spinning air

③

Heaviest rain

Updraft

TOP VIEW

SIDE VIEW

Rotating tube now upright

④

TOP VIEW

Tornados often found here

SIDE VIEW

Anvil cloud

Supercell up to 60,000 feet high

Wall cloud

Tornado   Hail   Rain

Postfrontal Thunderstorms

Most of the thunderstorms discussed have been alongside or ahead of fronts. Some occur long after a cold front has passed. This may happen with the passage of an area of low pressure high up in the atmosphere— what's called an *upper trough*. True to its name, a trough is a place where water (and air) collect, leading to the lifting motion that can set off thunderstorms. Along the West Coast of the United States and Canada, thunderstorms can also be triggered when the cooler, drier air following a cold front moves over the warmer ocean water of the Pacific. Just as air being heated by the ground will rise, so will air heated by warmer water. Postfrontal thunderstorms gain strength as they collide with the coastal mountain ranges that boost the warm air near the surface even higher. The following are the most important points to remember:

► If an upper trough is forecast to follow a cold front, it's likely that thunderstorms may develop, particularly along the west slopes of mountains.

► Such thunderstorms are most common along the coastal ranges of the western United States and Canada.

Thunderstorms are a bit like fingerprints; no two are exactly alike. Knowing their different forms and behavior and the words used to describe them will help you make more intelligent decisions based on forecasts before you leave home or what you see in the field. The next chapter presents some specific strategies to help you avoid or survive thunderstorms, including the four As of Thunderstorm Safety.

How coastal thunder or rain showers develop after a cold front moves through

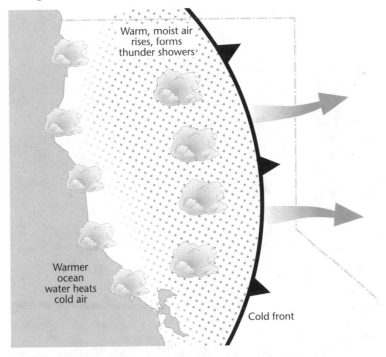

Warm, moist air rises, forms thunder showers

Warmer ocean water heats cold air

Cold front

TORNADOES

Tornadoes—or, as loosely called, "twisters"—produce the fastest winds on Earth. A few have been clocked to 300 miles per hour, traveled more than a hundred miles, and had funnels measuring more than a half mile wide! Fortunately, tornadoes of that magnitude are rare, but any tornado can kill, even the smallest ones. Some form as a thunderstorm's gust front kicks up air into a skinny, twisting, stringy funnel that lasts only a few minutes. The big ones are spawned by thunderstorm complexes. The same spin that keeps these massive storms going for hours also gives birth to tornadoes. Although twisters are more common in some areas, they can occur anywhere, including the mountains. A tornado in Salt Lake City, which is surrounded by the mountain ranges of northern Utah, ripped apart an outdoor sporting convention and killed one person.

Following are two important National Weather Service Watch and Warning definitions:

► *Tornado Watch:* Tornadoes are possible in your area.
► *Tornado Warning:* A tornado has been sighted or indicated by radar. Seek shelter immediately if a tornado warning is issued for your area and if the sky appears threatening.

Tornado (photo courtesy of NOAA)

Next are some clues to look for:

- Dark, sometimes greenish sky
- Rotating wall cloud beneath a thunderstorm
- Large hail
- Loud roar; can sound like a jet airplane or freight train
- Dust or debris kicked up on the ground

    Finally, remember these points:

- Hills, trees, clouds, or rain can hide tornadoes.
- Tornadoes may develop in areas where severe thunderstorm watches or warnings are posted. Stay alert, even though a tornado watch or warning hasn't been issued.

Features of a tornado

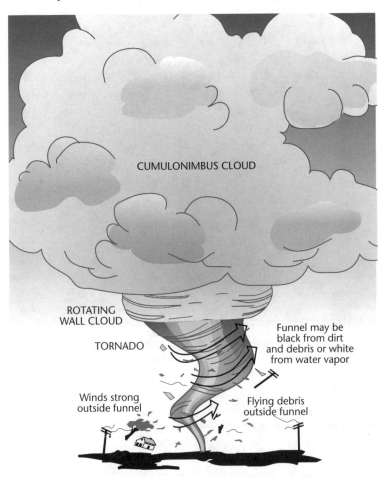

CUMULONIMBUS CLOUD

ROTATING
WALL CLOUD

TORNADO

Funnel may be
black from dirt
and debris or white
from water vapor

Winds strong
outside funnel

Flying debris
outside funnel

Lightning (photo courtesy of NOAA)

A GLOSSARY OF LIGHTNING

Ball Lightning: A rather rare type of lightning that usually looks like a shining, reddish ball, roughly 1 foot in diameter, which may appear to float in midair, hiss, and occasionally explode loudly. Ball—or globe lightning, as it's also called—may also move rapidly along solid objects or disappear without a sound.

Blue Jets: Pillars of blue light that skyrocket from the tops of thunderstorms at speeds of 200,000 miles per hour. Blue jets typically reach altitudes of 30 miles above the ground.

Heat Lightning: The luminous display of lightning too far away for its thunder to be heard. It's a misconception that heat lightning can occur in the absence of thunderstorms simply because of excessive heat.

Red Elves: Red disks of light that expand rapidly at altitudes of 60 miles above sea level and disappear as quickly as they appear. Generated by the electrical fields produced by intense lightning within and below the cloud.

Red Sprites: A fountain of red light erupting from the tops of nighttime thunderstorms, particularly in the Great Plains. Such displays are rather dim, but they may take on bizarre shapes and can extend from 18 to as much as 50 miles above sea level. They're created by the electrical fields generated by lightning within and below the cloud.

Rocket Lightning: A slower form of lightning that doesn't seem to be instantaneous, but rather moves like a skyrocket across the sky.

St. Elmo's Fire: Not actually a type of lightning, but the shining discharge of electricity from objects, usually pointed ones, such as the masts of ships. The name was given by Mediterranean sailors in honor of their patron saint, since it usually appeared as a violent thunderstorm was waning.

Sheet Lightning: Not actually a type of lightning, but the bright illumination of the cloud surrounding the lightning discharge.

CHAPTER 5
STRATEGIES FOR THUNDERSTORM SAFETY AND SURVIVAL

The trips richest in profound experience are based in joy at being at the mercy of a natural order that is at once part of you and greater than you.

The Winter Wilderness Companion, Alexandra and Garrett Conover

Be prepared.

The Boy Scout Motto

I was awakened by the slow, yet deliberate, roll of thunder. It was close enough that I could feel the shock waves. I listened for the rain, expecting heavy drops to plaster my tent, but there was none. Frequent lightning flashes interrupted the blackness of the night sky. There wasn't even much wind. My watch showed it was after midnight. Surprisingly, my wife and son continued to sleep though the late-night fireworks. We had pitched our tent in a rather exposed position, across the valley from Mount Rundle in the Canadian Rockies. That left me to wonder whether I should rouse them, break camp, and seek a more protected location. I began to time the interval between the lightning and the thunder that followed. It didn't change, which suggested the storm would keep its distance and that we would be safe where we were. I snuggled back into my sleeping bag, enjoying the sound and light show for perhaps another hour, and slowly drifted back to sleep. Our campsite remained dry all night.

Why did I decide to stay where I was? Was it pure laziness or thrill seeking or did the technique I used really indicate the thunderstorm was unlikely to pose a threat to our campsite? This chapter offers techniques you can use to maximize your safety. Those techniques will be easiest to remember and most effective if you make them part of a plan.

THE FOUR A'S OF THUNDERSTORM SAFETY

Success is more likely in any outdoor activity if you have and follow a plan. That's true in general about dealing with weather, and it's certainly true of dealing with thunderstorms. I've found a simple plan that has helped me avoid accidents, especially lightning accidents, during outings throughout the United States, Canada, and Europe. It contains four parts, which I call the four As of Thunderstorm Safety.

1. Anticipate
2. Assess
3. Act
4. Aid

1. Anticipate

The best strategy, of course, is to avoid being near thunderstorms in the first place. This means *anticipating* the risk. If you've read the previous chapters, you know how thunderstorms behave and that it's next to impossible to accurately predict where a bolt of lightning will strike next. *There's simply no defense for lightning.* Since so many variables are at play, it's foolish to consciously go out or stay out in a lightning storm if there's any alternative. While it's true that 80 percent of all victims of lightning strikes survive, one in four survivors suffer major aftereffects.

The best solution, therefore, is to *anticipate* the hazard *before* you're dangerously exposed. That's not always possible, but it's an important habit to develop before every outing. You begin anticipating by gathering information.

First, recognize what type of information is available. Formal weather watches, warnings, and forecasts are issued by the National Weather Service in the United States, and those official alerts and forecasts will be all you'll need *sometimes* to make an informed decision. Your search for guidance doesn't have to (and often shouldn't) end there. The following table presents the types of information available and where you can find them. In the following pages you'll find more specifics about each type of information and examples of how you can use the data to assess the threat of thunder and lightning in the backcountry.

Information Type	Source	Availability
Severe weather watches, warnings	National Weather Service	NOAA Weather Radio, TV and radio news, websites
Zone and state forecasts	National Weather Service, broadcast meteorologists	NOAA Weather Radio, TV and radio news, websites, newspapers
Extended outlook	National Weather Service, broadcast meteorologists	NOAA Weather Radio, TV and radio news, websites, newspapers
Satellite photos	National Weather Service	TV news, websites, newspapers
Weather radar	National Weather Service, broadcast meteorologists	TV news, websites
Weather observations	National Weather Service, private observers	NOAA Weather Radio, TV and radio news, websites
Private observations	State Patrol, Sheriff and Police Departments, State and National Park Rangers	Telephone or personal visit

The National Weather Service in the United States has developed several levels of alerts relating to thunderstorm activity: Severe Thunderstorm Watches, Severe Thunderstorm Warnings, Tornado Watches, Tornado Warnings, Flash Flood Watches, and Flash Flood Warnings. Weather services in other countries have similar alerts. Such warnings and watches should be the first elements on your checklist before heading into the backcountry. If *any* of these watches or warnings are posted for your destination, don't go. Following are the specific definitions for each:

▸ *Severe Thunderstorm Watch:* Conditions are favorable in the watch area for thunderstorms to produce wind gusts to 58 miles per hour or greater, hail ¾-inch or larger, or tornadoes. None have actually been spotted in the watch area. Such watches typically are issued for 4 to 6 hours at a time, and for a number of counties.

▸ *Severe Thunderstorm Warning:* A severe thunderstorm has been detected by radar, or by a trained spotter, or is imminent. Take cover immediately!

▸ *Tornado Watch:* Tornadoes are possible in the watch area. Remain alert for approaching storms.

▸ *Tornado Warning:* A tornado has been seen or indicated by weather radar. Move to a place of safety immediately.

▸ *Flash Flood Watch:* Flash flooding is possible in the watch area. Remain alert and be prepared to move to a safer location.

▸ *Flash Flood Warning:* Take action immediately to save yourself. You may have only seconds to act.

Using Watches and Warnings

If a watch or warning is posted for your destination, delay the trip or choose a different destination. Keep in mind that, by definition, the backcountry is a remote area, and radio reception will probably be poor. Don't hit the trail armed only with a radio and wishful thinking that you'll be able to receive a severe weather watch or warning in the backcountry. The time to act on such a watch or warning is before you leave home. Because of the short-term nature of these alerts, you'll need to get them from an up-to-date broadcast source such as radio or television, or from the Internet. In a local forecast given by NOAA Weather Radio, an Internet weather site, or a television or radio meteorologist, a typical watch would read like the following:

THE STORM PREDICTION CENTER HAS ISSUED A SEVERE THUNDERSTORM WATCH FOR PORTIONS OF

WESTERN AND CENTRAL ARIZONA
SOUTHWEST UTAH

EFFECTIVE THIS MONDAY AFTERNOON AND EVENING FROM
130 P.M. UNTIL 800 P.M. MST.

HAIL TO 2 INCHES IN DIAMETER... THUNDERSTORM WIND GUSTS
TO 60 MPH... AND DANGEROUS LIGHTNING ARE POSSIBLE IN
THESE AREAS.

THE SEVERE THUNDERSTORM WATCH AREA IS ALONG AND 65
STATUTE MILES EAST AND WEST OF A LINE FROM 60 MILES
NORTHEAST OF SAINT GEORGE UTAH TO 55 MILES SOUTH OF
GILA BEND ARIZONA.

REMEMBER... A SEVERE THUNDERSTORM WATCH MEANS
CONDITIONS ARE FAVORABLE FOR SEVERE THUNDERSTORMS
IN AND CLOSE TO THE WATCH AREA. PERSONS IN THESE AREAS
SHOULD BE ON THE LOOKOUT FOR THREATENING WEATHER
CONDITIONS AND LISTEN FOR LATER STATEMENTS AND
POSSIBLE WARNINGS.

The specific information given in such a watch or warning helps users assess the likely impact of the expected thunderstorms, flash floods, or tornadoes on their planned outing. The next step after checking for short-term watches or warnings should be to examine the longer-term potential for thunderstorms, which would typically be available in either a state or zone forecast. The zone forecasts issued by the National Weather Service typically extend over a 5-day period and cover a specific geographic area or collection of counties or cities that are expected to have similar weather. The forecast language will be much more specific for the first 2 days than for the next 3. Again, TV and radio broadcasts and the Internet are the best sources. The zone or state forecast also offers an opportunity to see how well the forecasters are doing. Check the forecast a few days before your trip, and then check what happens the next day. Was the forecast correct? If so, you can have more confidence in the forecast for your trip. If it was wrong, you'll want to regard the forecast with more caution. A typical zone forecast looks like this:

SOUTHWEST ARIZONA/SOUTHEAST CALIFORNIA ZONE
FORECASTS
NATIONAL WEATHER SERVICE PHOENIX AZ
345 P.M. MST MON FEB 21 2000

WEST CENTRAL DESERTS–SOUTHWEST DESERTS—
345 P.M. MST MON FEB 21 2000

... SEVERE THUNDERSTORM WATCH UNTIL 8P.M....
.TONIGHT... SCATTERED SHOWERS AND THUNDERSTORMS... A 40
PERCENT CHANCE OF SHOWERS... FOLLOWED BY PARTIAL
CLEARING AFTER MIDNIGHT. LOWS IN THE MID TO UPPER 40S.
SOUTHWEST TO WEST WINDS 10 TO 20 MPH IN THE
EVENING... BECOMING 5 TO 15 MPH BY MIDNIGHT.
.TUESDAY... BECOMING MOSTLY SUNNY. HIGHS IN THE UPPER 60S
TO NEAR 70. WEST WINDS 5 TO 15 MPH.
.TUESDAY NIGHT...MOSTLY CLEAR. LOWS IN THE 40S.
.WEDNESDAY... INCREASING CLOUDINESS. HIGHS IN THE LOW
70S.

.<	TEMPERATURE	/	PRECIPITATION
BOUSE	45 71 46 72	/	40 0 0 0
TACNA	45 71 47 72	/	40 0 0 0

... EXTENDED FORECAST...
.THURSDAY AND FRIDAY... A CHANCE OF SHOWERS. LOWS
MOSTLY IN THE 40S. HIGHS IN THE UPPER 60S TO NEAR 70.
.SATURDAY... PARTLY CLOUDY. LOWS IN THE UPPER 40S TO LOW
50S. HIGHS IN THE LOW 70S.

The text portion of the previous forecast is self-explanatory. The temperatures listed for Bouse and Tacna are specific forecasts for each forecast period—in this example, that's Monday night, Tuesday, Tuesday night, and Wednesday. The numbers given for precipitation are the forecaster's estimates of the probability that measurable precipitation will fall at each location for each forecast period. For example, the probability of measurable precipitation is forecast as 40 percent for Monday night, but zero afterward. Not only is this forecast useful if you're planning an outing Monday evening or Tuesday, but also for the later period. If the forecast is correct and Tuesday is a nice day, you can head out with a greater measure of confidence that the latter part of the week will be nice. If Tuesday brings showers and nasty weather, you can assume that the atmosphere has forecasters guessing, and you'd be wise to plan conservatively and keep a watchful eye on the sky. In fact, although studies indicate forecast accuracy continues to improve, long-range forecasts are the least accurate. It's wise to plan for the worst and hope for the best.

Satellite photos are available on television weathercasts and on many weather-related websites. They offer you a chance to look for visual indicators of thunderstorms or the cloud formations that often precede thunderstorms. In the satellite image that follows, a band of clouds marks a cold front. As it runs into warm, moist air ahead, heavy showers and even thunder showers may develop. In fact such thunderstorms may develop in advance of a cold front in a squall line.

Sometimes, the clues are more subtle. Small puffs of clouds, like those in the following satellite photo, may develop into full-blown thunder or rain showers later in the day as the land heats up. If cooler air has moved in, but sun is heating the slopes and satellite photos show little puffs of cumulus clouds, full-blown cumulo-nimbus clouds may follow later in the day.

Radar used to be a tool strictly available to meteorologists, but thanks to the World Wide Web it's available to just about everyone with a computer and an Internet connection. The colors in the display vary with the intensity of the precipitation. Blue represents the lightest precipitation, red and purple the heaviest. Keep in mind that radar signals can only

Typical satellite image available on the web (photo courtesy of NOAA)

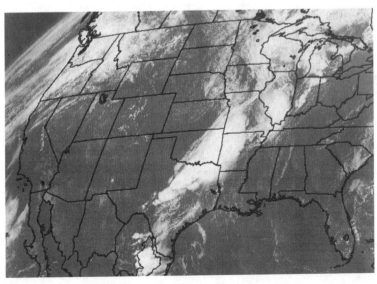

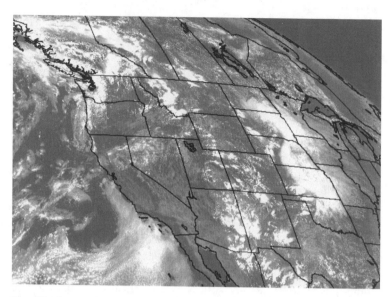

Satellite image showing cumulus clouds developing into cumulonimbus over the southwest and the Rockies (photo courtesy of NOAA)

detect what's in the direct path of the radar signal. Precipitation on the opposite side of a mountain range may not show up, or at least not very well, because the mountain will block part, if not all, of the radar signal. Also, the farther that precipitation is falling from the radar, the higher the likelihood that the radar signal will strike only part of the cloud and miss details on what's happening closer to the ground.

It's helpful to check weather observations from the area you're planning to visit, but it's also important to recognize, particularly in wilderness areas, that official weather observation stations can be few and far between. That caution aside, such observations can offer valuable clues on current weather and weather trends, particularly if checked several times over a period of hours. The following is an excerpt from the website of the National Weather Service's Denver office:

COLORADO STATE WEATHER ROUNDUP
NATIONAL WEATHER SERVICE DENVER CO
1100 P.M. MST MON FEB 21 2000

NOTE: "FAIR" INDICATES FEW OR NO CLOUDS BELOW 12,000 FEET WITH NO SIGNIFICANT WEATHER AND/OR OBSTRUCTIONS TO VISIBILITY.

CITY	SKY/ WX	TEMP	DEWPT	RH	WIND	PRES	REMARKS
... NORTHWEST COLORADO...							
CRAIG	FAIR	31	28	88	W5	29.97F	WCI 28
HAYDEN	N/A	34	27	75	SE12	30.02F	WCI 19
MEEKER	CLOUDY	33	27	78	NE7	29.96F	WCI 25

The preceding report indicates no precipitation (i.e., "WX"). *Temperature* is self-explanatory, while *dew point* is a measure of the amount of moisture in the atmosphere, specifically the temperature at which the atmosphere will be saturated. RH stands for *relative humidity,* a measure of how much moisture the atmosphere is holding versus what it's capable of holding, expressed as a percentage. There doesn't need to be 100 percent RH at an observation site to produce rain; remember, the RH reported is at the ground, while the precipitation comes from the sky. *Wind* gives the direction the wind is coming from and speed in miles per hour, while pressure gives current *air pressure* in inches and tendency over time (F is falling, S is steady, R is rising). The remarks can describe anything the observer thinks is important or useful; in this example, WCI stands for *wind chill index* and the wind chill for Craig, Colorado, is 28.

Recognizing the lack of observation stations in backcountry or wilderness areas, an excellent way to fill in the gaps is to contact local law

Radar image from National Weather Service website, Juneau office (photo courtesy of NOAA)

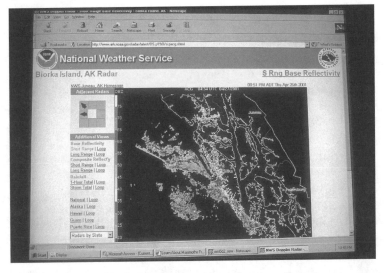

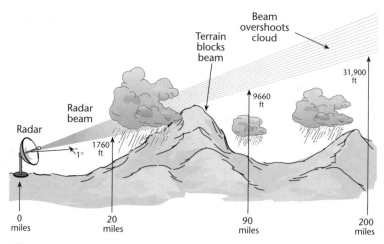

The impact of hills, mountains, and distance on radar signals and radar detection of precipitation

enforcement offices via their non-emergency numbers or rangers at county, state, or national parks. If asked politely, most will be happy to give you at least a summary of local weather. After all, well-informed hikers, climbers, skiers, fishers, kayakers, and other lovers of the great outdoors are less likely to get into situations requiring rescues that put rangers or law enforcement personnel at risk!

2. Assess

If anticipating the risk of thunderstorms before leaving home is the first step toward backcountry safety, *assessing* the threat while *in* the back-country is the second step. This involves assessing the threat from the sky and assessing elements of the environment around you that may add to or subtract from that threat.

No academic degree in meteorology is needed to realize that seeing lightning and hearing thunder mean you're in danger. The goal is to rec-ognize clues that will give you a little more time to react. If thunder and lightning are already present, though, ask these two questions right away: How far away is the thunderstorm? Where is it headed?

If you can see lightning or hear thunder, seek shelter immediately. Don't wait for the rain. If you can hear thunder, the storm is probably within 6 to 10 miles, and you should take prompt action to protect your-self and others. However, the absence of thunder isn't a guarantee that the storm is more than 6 miles away. Noise or intervening ridges may prevent you from hearing thunder until the storm is within 2 or 3 miles.

If you can see the lightning bolt, the storm is typically within 15 miles, but this depends upon your vantage point, visibility, and other factors specific to your locale. The distance between successive strokes can be 3 to 5 miles or more; lightning has struck as far as 10 miles away from rainfall. That means though it may not be raining at your campsite, you could still be struck by lightning. *And remember this:* A thunderstorm can easily cover a lot of ground between lightning bolts.

If you can see lightning and hear thunder, assess the threat by using the *flash/bang principle:* Once you see the flash, start timing. Stop timing when you hear the bang. Next, divide that number by 5. A count of 15, for example, means lightning is 3 miles away, a count of 10 means lightning is 2 miles away, a count of 5 means you're in big trouble. The reason the flash/bang principle works is that lightning moves almost at the speed of light (186,000 miles per second), essentially instantaneously. (The speed of sound is much slower, at 1129 feet per second, or approximately 770 miles per hour.) The actual speed varies with temperature. The speed given here is for 68°F (20°C). In 5 seconds, the sound would have traveled 5 x 1129 feet or 5645 feet, which is very close to 1 mile (5280 feet).

The sky often offers clues long before the boom of thunder and flash of lightning. The following series of photographs shows a common sequence in the development of thunder showers in the mountains. First, small and fluffy cumulus clouds appear. Next, the small cumulus clouds

The effect of distance from a thunderstorm at which you can see lightning, hear thunder, or be hit by lightning

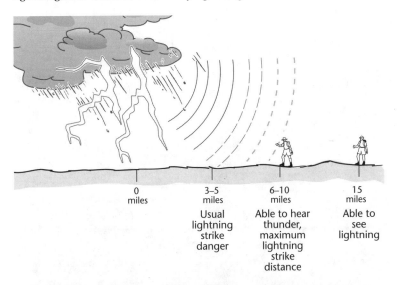

0 miles	3–5 miles	6–10 miles	15 miles
	Usual lightning strike danger	Able to hear thunder, maximum lightning strike distance	Able to see lightning

expand into much larger clouds that resemble heads of cauliflower. In less than an hour, these clouds may develop into full-blown cumulonimbus, producing, at a minimum, heavy rain or snow showers and gusty winds, and possibly thunder and lightning. Watch also for the hard-edged cauliflowerlike shape of growing cumulus to give way to a softer, fuzzy outline higher up. That signals the development of ice crystals that precede thunder and lightning.

The growth of cumulus clouds into cumulonimbus; Glacier National Park, Montana

If the thunderstorms are produced by the movement of a cold front or squall line, the first clue may be a dark line of clouds on the horizon, the telltale anvil cloud or clouds up high, followed by a sudden gust of wind as the storm's gust front spreads out ahead of it. Recognize that with this type of thunderstorm or line of thunderstorms, there's no time to lose in seeking shelter. However, if the thunderstorms are embedded near a warm or occluded front, other clouds may make it difficult to see them coming. Then it's back to using the flash/bang principle.

After assessing clues from what you can see in the sky, it's time to assess your environment on the ground or water. What you're standing on or near, even what you're wearing, will determine how likely you are to be struck, and if you're struck, what your chance of survival will be. Long before much was known about how thunderstorms formed, people did recognize such storms were dangerous and attempted to come up with some safety rules. Some are laughable, some are quaint, but some have a factual basis.

Branches of the hazel tree, when gathered on Palm Sunday and kept alive in water, will protect a house from thunder and lightning. (England.)

Imagine the reaction of your hiking pals when you take to carrying hazel tree branches in a portable vase!

Thunder curdles cream and lightning sours milk.

If you're near a thunderstorm, sour milk is the least of your worries!

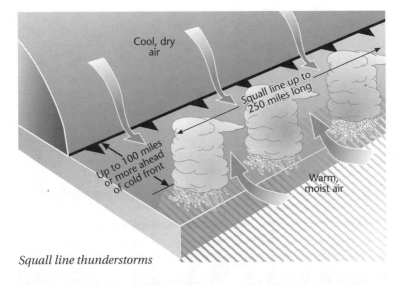

Squall line thunderstorms

*Early beliefs about thunder-
storm safety: testing the
effectiveness of hazel branches
as a lightning deterrant*

Lightning never strikes twice.

The Empire State Building is struck twenty times or more per year!

A foam pad will insulate you from lightning that strikes the ground.

Wrong! It takes 10,000 volts to create a 1-inch spark. A lightning bolt represents millions of volts, and a spark can jump 10 to 20 feet.

But in some old "rules" there's a shade of truth:

Beware of oak; it draws the stroke.
Avoid an ash; it courts the flash.
Creep under the hawthorn; it will save you from harm.

Believe it or not, test plots in both the United States and Germany found real differences in the frequency of lightning strikes among types of trees.

Trees Struck in 1 Year/United States

Oak/48	Pine/33
Spruce/5	Beech/1

Trees Struck in 1 Year/Germany

Oak/56	Ash/20
Pine/4	Beech/0

Obviously it's difficult to control all the possible factors that could account for these differences, but there are some potential explanations. Trees growing in sandy soil, with a taproot extending into groundwater, such as oak or ash, would be more likely to attract lightning than trees with shallow, horizontal roots. That's also true of tall trees in the open or near the border of woods. Will there be a new saying, "Take cover under a spruce, and lightning will be less likely to cook your goose"? I believe there are better strategies to follow. It begins with asking some questions about your environment.

Questions for Assessing Lightning Risk

1. Am I in the open?
2. Am I near or on isolated, tall objects?
3. Am I on or near water?
4. Am I near, wearing, or holding metal objects?
5. Am I feeling a tingling sensation or hearing a buzzing noise?

3. Act

Once you've assessed your risk, it's time to act—fast!

Am I in the open?

If you're in the open, seek a more sheltered location. If a car or metal shed is available, get in; lightning travels along the outside of metal objects. Just be certain not to touch metal handles and such until the thunderstorm and risk of lightning strikes are definitely over. A cave offers protection only if it is deep. Ground currents can jump from the roof of a shallow cave to you and then to the floor. Wait at least 30 minutes after the last thunder or lightning to resume activity. If shelter isn't available, get low. If you can't move, crouch down, with feet close together and hands over your ears for protection from close thunder, which can damage hearing. There's no evidence that standing on your pack, clothing, or sleeping pad will protect you from ground currents. Do not lie down, and don't stand close to others; if you're in a group, spread out and remain a

Key lightning risk factors:

"Am I in the open?"

"Am I near or on isolated, tall objects?"

"Am I on or near water?"

minimum of 15 feet away from other people. It's not true that standing near a taller person will reduce your danger of being struck!

Am I near isolated, tall objects?

Don't seek refuge under isolated trees. The highest object will tend to attract the stroke of lightning. If possible, seek groups of trees or shrubs of similar height. If the lone tree is the only choice of refuge, move away from it and seek the lowest ground available, following the tips for safety in open locations. If you're on a high, exposed ridge or peak, try to climb down as quickly as is safely possible. If low, rolling hills are nearby, seek refuge in a low spot. Such terrain is especially common on golf courses or along shorelines.

Am I near water?

If you're near water, move away. If you're in the water, get out. It's that simple and that important. Not only is the lightning a hazard, but gusty winds could churn up the water and swamp your canoe or small boat. Even wet, marshy ground can increase your risk of being hit by lightning.

Am I near, wearing, or holding metal objects?

Metal objects are like miniature lightning rods: They draw the stroke. If you're near, wearing, or holding something made of metal, you're part of that lightning rod. If a thunderstorm approaches, you want to get as far away as possible from metal objects. If you're a climber, this means ditch your

Example of safe, crouching posture if caught in the open during a thunderstorm

pack (it may have a metal frame), drop your ice ax, and remove your crampons. If you're carrying protection on a sling for rock climbing (camming devices, chocks, carabiners, and the like), take off the sling and move away. If your tent is staked with metal pegs, get away since a tent offers no protection. This also applies to graphite objects, such as fishing rods or tent poles. If you're a golfer, get away from your clubs! Don't hold onto a metal-tipped umbrella either; it's better to get soaked than struck!

Am I feeling a tingling sensation or hearing a buzzing noise?

A tingling sensation, particularly on your scalp or the hair on your arms indicates movement of electricity, probably from the ground up toward the descending leader from the cloud that will become the visible lightning bolt. A loud buzzing noise or the smell of ozone are also danger signs, as is a bluish glow around rocks or a companion. Move immediately! And if you see a friend's hair sticking out or up, get them to move, too!

4. Aid

What if a companion is hit by lightning? Can you safely help him or her? What should you do? This section isn't intended as a first-aid primer (and is no substitute for formal first-aid training), but it will touch on some key principles that relate to lightning injuries.

Make no more casualties.

One injury has already occurred; don't add another by putting yourself at high risk if the storm is still raging. If you're within 3 to 5 miles of the storm, you're still within the prime lightning danger zone. Before attempting to help a victim, plan how you can minimize your exposure before you move.

Remember that the victim can't hurt you.

Once you've decided to provide aid, recognize that the victim doesn't carry a charge. The only way you can get hurt is by another lightning strike.

If possible, send for assistance.

Seeking assistance obviously depends upon your location and circumstances. If you're deep in the wilderness, you're on your own. If you're not alone and within a couple miles of assistance, send one person to seek help. Are you carrying a cell phone? If so, call 911. If you have a radio, use it to summon help.

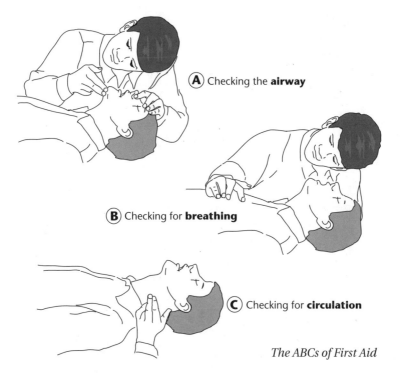

(A) Checking the **airway**

(B) Checking for **breathing**

(C) Checking for **circulation**

The ABCs of First Aid

First treat those who appear to be dead.
Remember the ABCs of first aid: Check for an open *airway,* check to see whether the victim is *breathing,* and then check for evidence of *circulation* (a pulse). Be patient in checking for evidence of breathing and circulation for at least 20 to 30 seconds. If you can't detect breathing or circulation, begin CPR. If you haven't completed CPR training or if it's been a while since you've practiced, sign up now for a new or refresher course. It takes so little time to learn, and it can make a big difference later.

Move the victim if lightning is still a threat.
If your position (or that of the victim) is still dangerous, look for a less exposed position and move. In most lightning strikes, fractures or major bleeding are unlikely unless the victim suffered a fall or was thrown a distance. If there's no evidence of breathing or circulation, administer two quick breaths, then move the victim to reduce the threat of another lightning strike.

Treat for hypothermia.

Odds are, if the victim was struck by lightning, he or she is also wet from the rain. Put a protective layer between the victim and the ground to diminish the chance of hypothermia and cover the casualty with any available clothing to keep them warm.

Lightning is a thunderstorm's biggest threat to safety, but it isn't the only threat. The following chapter explores the first of the other three dangers.

CHAPTER 6
THE INVISIBLE THREAT OF THUNDERSTORM WINDS

I have heard the singing in many places, but I seem to hear it best in the wilderness lake country of the Quetico–Superior, where travel is still by pack and canoe over the ancient trails of the Indians and voyageurs.

I have heard it on misty migration nights when the dark has been alive with the high calling of birds, and in the rapids where the air has been full of their rushing thunder. I have caught it at dawn when the mists were moving out of the bays, and on cold winter nights when the stars seemed close enough to touch. But the music can even be heard in the soft guttering of an open fire or in the beat of rain on a tent.

The Singing Wilderness, Sigurd Olson

"The singing wilderness"—that was conservationist Sigurd Olson's affectionate nickname for the north woods of Minnesota. In a collection of essays by that name, he evoked the gentle symphony of sounds that had brought him decades of contentment in the lakes and forests of the North.

Olson spent his lifetime capturing the magic of this area in words, and photographer Jim Brandenburg has devoted much of his life to capturing it with film. One of the finest nature photographers of our age, Brandenburg's home and studio are tucked in the north woods on the shores of Moose Lake, just south of the Boundary Waters Canoe Area Wilderness, which is part of the boreal forest and the Canadian shield. Soils are thin, in places a foot deep or less. That's why the fragrant jack, red, and white pines, as well as the black spruce, have a shallow but lacelike root structure. However, this successful adaptation for capturing water and nutrients leaves the trees highly sensitive to wind.

But wind wasn't a problem for Brandenburg on the morning of July 4, 1999. He took advantage of the still air early that Sunday, photographing wild orchids in an old growth forest near his home. The slightest breeze, even the most minute of ground vibrations, can throw flowers out of focus. On this morning the air was dead calm, if also heavy with

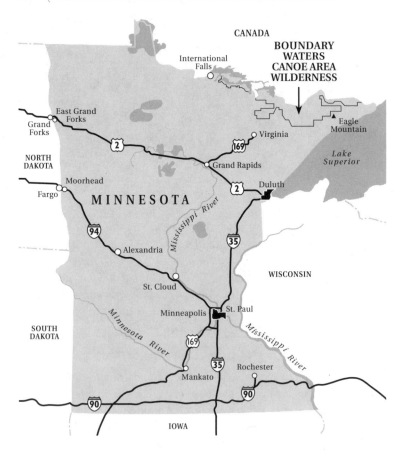

The Boundary Waters Canoe Area Wilderness in northern Minnesota

heat and humidity. Brandenburg was lost in thought, drawing both on his technical skills and personal vision to capture on film the delicate essence of the flowers.

He didn't notice it at first, but each succeeding photograph required longer time exposures to capture the necessary light. It was close to noon when Brandenburg finally looked up; he was startled by the darkness of the sky, which was almost as dark as dusk. His wife became uncomfortable and urged Brandenburg to follow her back home; experience had taught both that it's time to seek shelter when stifling heat and humidity are followed by black skies.

In Duluth, 130 miles south, meteorologist Ed Shimon was carefully watching the radar over the shoulder of his boss. An already large thunderstorm system was beginning to expand, stretching north to south as it swept first through Cass County, then Itasca, and then St. Louis. It was perhaps 50 miles west of where Brandenburg was considering whether to pack up his cameras, and it was moving fast.

Shimon had been called into work at the National Weather Service forecast office earlier that morning. There was already a severe thunderstorm watch, and that meant a need for extra help. A cold front was draped from southern Ontario through the northwest corner of Minnesota down into eastern South Dakota, with hot muggy air to the east and cooler, drier air to the west. With the heating from the summer sun, there was little question thunderstorms would develop. The proof was already on the radar screen in front of him. Shimon's task that day, as warning coordinator, was to decide just how severe they would be, where they'd move, and when and how soon he'd need to issue warnings. Observers near Fargo, North Dakota, had earlier reported thunderstorm winds of 90 miles per hour. Then came a report from Hibbing of trees down, with winds there gusting to 80 miles per hour. The thunderstorm continued to intensify and enlarge on radar. The south end was advancing toward Duluth, prompting Shimon to call the 911 center and urge police to evacuate a Fourth of July event at the harbor. It was going to be a hectic day.

Pete Esposito was far enough to the east that skies were still partly cloudy. It wasn't thunderstorms that occupied his mind that morning; it was the static between four fifteen-year-olds that bothered him. Five days into an eight-day canoe trip in the Boundary Waters wilderness, he felt exhausted. The four scouts and two fathers he was guiding needed more assistance and demanded more attention than any group he had led from the Boy Scout Northern Tier High Adventure Base. No sooner had he emerged from his tent than he was greeted by demands of "When do we eat?" There was no question that Esposito was there to guide them and assist in developing their outdoor skills, but it was difficult to do either when participation was both minimal and grudging. There was constant tension; three of the boys consistently picked on the fourth; Esposito had to serve both as referee and counselor. Plus there were a couple of incidents that were unsettling if not outright weird. Just as they settled into camp the day before, one scout abruptly pointed to a particularly stout pine and announced, "Before we leave, I bet that tree will fall." Later, after a relaxing north woods evening of fresh northern pike and smallmouth bass panfried over a campfire, with northern lights dancing in a star-filled sky, the peace had been shattered by a bloodcurdling shriek from the scouts' tent. "Mom, Mom, Mom, Mom!" Esposito's heart jumped into his throat and blood pounded in his ears. The scout normally the object of bullying was outside with him. Undoubtedly the other three had turned on each other. He raced to their tent, ready to separate the offenders, but as he peered in, no one was moving. In fact, all looked asleep. As abruptly as the shrieking began, it stopped. No one woke up.

A good night's sleep helped erase some of the stress. He'd promised them a hike to the spectacular falls on Eddy Lake, and it looked like a perfect day for the trip. The expanse of blue sky was punctuated by only a few small white cumulus clouds. For the moment, with breakfast done and demands satisfied, the twenty-year-old college junior needed some time to himself. There certainly wasn't any rush; this was the Fourth of July. The group had the whole day and another night at this camp, so Esposito dove into the lake and enjoyed the cool water, the serene beauty of the north woods, and some rare silence. It was a delay he'd later realize had saved their lives.

Meanwhile, Brandenburg had packed up his equipment, returned home, and was lashing a canoe to the top of his car. As the blackness increased, he carefully checked each knot to make certain it would be secure enough to hold the canoe against the thunderstorm winds he knew would soon arrive. As the rain began falling, Brandenburg looked up at the sky, thinking, "Well, here's a good storm!" He liked the spectacle of a thunderstorm. It was still quiet, aside from the drumming of raindrops. He finished securing the canoe and headed indoors.

Topographic map of Eddy Lake, Boundary Waters Canoe Area Wilderness (courtesy of McKenzie Maps)

It was anything but quiet at the National Weather Service office in Duluth. Calls were flooding in: wind observations, damage reports, requests for updates. The thunderstorm looked horrible on the radar. The north end was both expanding and intensifying, colors changing with each new scan. The adrenaline in Shimon and his colleagues was pumping. All had gone through simulated severe weather drills a few months before, but this was no drill. The staff was working together well, old warnings cancelled, new warnings posted and promptly issued as the storm swept eastward. There was more behind their sense of urgency than the ominous radar display; they knew that people were out in the path of this monster—were they getting the warnings? All the meteorologists recognized that their forecast area included the Boundary Waters Canoe Area Wilderness, and that reception of NOAA Weather Radio there was limited at best. The linear thunderstorm echo was beginning to bend into a bow shape and was now racing straight through the wilderness. Shimon and the radar operator knew this meant trouble. It was a classic signature of extreme thunderstorm winds. The phones were ringing nonstop with more reports of damage, power outages, and telephone lines down. New warnings were issued, along with more phone calls to alert police and other groups. The radar's wind mode now indicated winds aloft of 100 miles per hour. The damage had to be incredible.

Brandenburg could hear the roar as the wind hit shortly after he closed the door, followed by the snapping of tree limbs. He turned to look outside just as the trees began falling, one after another. They were huge old growth pines and spruce, some breaking, others torn up by the roots. Six-foot waves built in seconds on Moose Lake, and treetops ripped off by the hurricane-force wind flew 30 to 40 feet through the air. Brandenburg was in shock; he had just finished building his home and studio. He could do absolutely nothing other than head for the basement with his wife.

Esposito had finished his swim and walked back to his tent to dry off. A few raindrops began to fall slowly, but there wasn't even a distant roll of thunder. The sky was black, and seconds later the rain began pouring down in sheets. The scouts were only 10 feet away, and all quickly dived into their tent. Esposito scouted the campsite, then ducked into his tent, pulled out his journal and began to write. He was accustomed to north woods thunderstorms; they were typically over as fast as they started. When his entire tent was lifted off the ground suddenly, Esposito thought for a second that the scouts might be playing a prank, but he quickly realized it was a massive gust of wind. Goose bumps puckered his skin; it sounded like a freight train was approaching. He stood up, ripped open the tent's rain fly, and looked out. It was now black as midnight, with the rain pouring so hard he couldn't even see the scouts' tent a few steps away. Trees started snapping and falling. Esposito screamed, "Guys, get out of your tent!" He knew they had to get to the lakeshore, away from the trees. Before he could open his mouth again, a 60-foot pine fell, the very one that the scout had pointed out earlier, with branches grazing his face and the huge trunk slamming directly on the scouts' tent.

Esposito half ran, half flew to the tree. "Get it off, get it off," he called, but the wind tore the words out of his mouth. Golf-ball-size hail began beating on his back, but a rush of adrenaline flooded his muscles with strength. He actually felt himself lifting the trunk. Two scouts crawled out; two others were still trapped inside. Esposito was beside himself, not wanting to imagine their condition, but unable not to.

He turned to look toward the tent occupied by the two fathers, startled to see the two men literally rip through the side fabric and race toward their sons still trapped inside. Just seconds after they emerged, six trees fell on their tent. It was never seen again. The whole forest seemed to be coming down around them. Together, they lifted the pine off the scout tent and pulled the boys out. Both were alive, but obviously in pain. Esposito pulled everyone he could get his hands on toward the water, now whipped into a frenzy by the wind. The waves had to be 10 to 12 feet high.

Esposito was waist deep in water when he felt a hand grab his arm. One father motioned toward two massive, fallen trees. The other father and scouts were huddled behind the rootballs, caked with dirt and rocks, holding onto the roots for dear life. The wind continued to rise, branches flying, hitting Esposito's back as though an archer had fired them from a bow. Oddly, Esposito didn't feel a thing; he just kept gripping the roots with all his might. He raised his head to check on the scouts. Their faces were contorted into wind-drowned screams of terror and drained of any color—it was like looking at ghosts. Impossibly, the wind continued to build, trying to lift them off the ground. Esposito was convinced they were going to die. He ripped off the gold crucifix he wore on a chain around his neck and began to pray, "Our Father, Who art in heaven. . . . " He saw the scouts' mouths moving and knew they were praying, too. All he could hear was the intense thunder of the wind and falling trees. The sky was now colored a sickly green. Esposito waited for a tornado to arrive.

Amazingly, no tornado came. Perhaps 30 minutes after the first raindrops fell, the wind stopped. It didn't feel like a half hour, though; it seemed like a day, even a week. As the little group stood up stiffly, they saw that the forest was shattered. Every tree had fallen, been uprooted, or had the top 30 to 40 feet sheared off. The scouts, their fathers, and Esposito were in shock. Trees had fallen on every part of their campsite, except Esposito's tent; only two poles were bent, and the tent was still standing exactly where he had jumped out of it.

By then, the storm had moved out of the National Weather Service's Duluth County warning area. Shimon had cancelled the last of the severe thunderstorm warnings for his area as the storm swept into Ontario, Canada, and he felt a great heaviness. The need for focused effort was over, the pressure was off, and without the sustained rush of adrenaline, exhaustion seized him. Shimon and his colleagues felt like they'd been through a fifteen-round fight, but all were proud of their teamwork, the way they'd functioned under pressure. They could only guess at the extent of the damage and hope their work had made a difference.

Back at Eddy Lake, light rain began to fall on the small group. Esposito moved to check the two scouts who had been trapped in the tent. One had an injured ankle, the other a broken collarbone—one entire side of the latter scout's body was purple. If the forecasters in Duluth felt as though they'd been through a fifteen-round fight, the group of scouts looked like it. Each was soaked, shivering, and rapidly becoming hypothermic, but they were all thankful to be alive. It was time to assess their situation and attempt to signal rescuers or make a plan to get back to the Boy Scout High Adventure Base on Moose Lake. That would require all of them to come together as a group, something that Esposito knew had been a challenge up to this point. He and the fathers salvaged as many dry and usable clothes and blankets as possible and wrapped everyone up. Esposito tried sending out a call for help on the radio, but there was no response; they were probably too low to get a signal out. Still shivering, he climbed into one of the miraculously undamaged canoes and paddled across the lake toward the falls, where he might have better luck establishing contact. The water was blasting out of the head of the falls, blowing through a 300-foot-wide stretch of broken timber that just a few hours ago had been old growth forest. The devastation was more complete than he ever could have imagined. Esposito shivered again—not from the ebbing hypothermia, but from the stark realization that if his group had made the trip to the falls that morning, they'd all be dead. He grimly tried the radio again; still no answer.

Paddling back to the campsite under a sky that was darkening again with tinges of green, Esposito loaded everyone into the two remaining canoes with whatever supplies they could locate and led them to a more protected cove. One scout was still unable to speak. The two scouts with broken bones began to feel more pain. Floatplanes appeared overhead, and each time Esposito or one of the uninjured scouts would paddle into open water and attempt to signal for help. No plane gave any sign of

Downed trees along Eddy Lake from the July 4, 1999 storm
(photo by Pete Esposito)

recognition. They needed a better way to signal. There was no shortage of downed timber, so everyone pitched together to cut limbs and trunks into usable pieces and built a huge bonfire, tossing pieces of tent and ruined gear into the flames to make it smoke. Finally, about 7:30 P.M., they heard the drone of another floatplane getting louder. Anyone who could move raced out, flapping yellow raingear to signal. The plane banked, circled, reduced power, and landed. Esposito's group gathered whatever personal items they could and hobbled toward the shore where the pilot had beached the plane.

"What happened?" Esposito asked the pilot. The pilot responded, "I don't know, but it's bad, stretching as far back as your base. Everything is devastated, and this has to be the hardest hit spot of all." Esposito peered into the small floatplane and saw passengers with obvious injuries. "We have two injuries—one with a broken collarbone, the other with a bad ankle. A tree fell on them in their tent," Esposito informed the pilot. The pilot and a medic looked at the boys, provided some additional first aid, and then delivered the bad news that Esposito expected. "We only have room for one." "Can you come back for us tomorrow?" Esposito asked. The pilot said grimly, "We have three days' worth of medical evacuations—you'll have to get yourself out."

After forlornly watching the floatplane take off, the little group spent one more wet night at the lake. At 10:00 P.M., the sky lit up with lightning, flashes simultaneously hitting both sides of the lake, the thunder shaking the cold ground beneath them. Esposito spent some of his sleepless hours mentally reviewing CPR principles in case anyone was struck by lightning.

Shortly after daybreak, the exhausted group stiffly assembled around what was left of the campsite and set off on their epic return trip to Moose Lake. Taking turns carrying the scout with the broken ankle, struggling over or around piles of downed trees, wading waist deep through a slurry of mud and water, some portages that ordinarily would take 10 minutes between lakes took an hour and a half or more. Even the paddles across lakes offered little relief; the group then became easy if unwilling targets for vast clouds of insatiable mosquitoes and blackflies. Eight hours after setting out, the small group finally beached their canoes and numbly walked into the BSA High Adventure Base. It had been more adventure than they had ever expected or wanted, but they all came out alive.

Incredibly, there wasn't a single fatality anywhere in Minnesota from the storm. Residents of Ontario and Quebec, where the storm was responsible for several deaths, weren't as fortunate.

Anyone who's experienced a thunderstorm knows it can produce gusty winds. Yet who expects one to be of a magnitude to level whole stretches of forest? There's no question that the Boundary Waters storm was an unusually intense one, but National Weather Service records for that very same month, July 1999, illustrate that damaging, life-threatening winds are frequent thunderstorm hazards.

Clusters and lines of thunderstorms developed during the early evening over western New York and pushed into the Finger Lakes and then through the Western Catskills during the mid to late evening hours. These thunderstorms packed strong wind gusts in excess of 60 mph as they raced across the area uprooting trees. Several boats were overturned in Owasco Lake, and at approximately 8:30 P.M. a four-year-old girl drowned underneath a capsized pontoon boat.
Delaware County, New York, July 3, 1999

A severe thunderstorm with wind gusts near 60 mph moved over Lake Powell just north of Page, Arizona. The storm produced 8–12 foot swells. . . . Warnings were issued well in advance of the storm, so many boats were beached to prepare for the storm. Some boats did not make it, however, and two were sunk.
Kane County, Utah, July 27, 1999

A mesoscale convective complex consisting of a cluster of thunderstorms moved across northern New York and northern Vermont during the early morning hours . . . a person camping in a tent on a raft was blown away by thunderstorm winds. The tent became submerged and entangled in the water and the camper drowned.

Orleans County, Vermont, July 5, 1999

Only a handful of the cases reported in *Storm Data* are published by the National Climatic Data Center. Each case illustrates—as does the Boundary Waters storm—the need to understand the hazard posed by thunderstorm winds and to have an effective strategy to increase the odds you'll make it through alive. In brief, use the same four steps discussed in Chapter 5: anticipate, assess, act, and aid.

1. Anticipate

To anticipate means to understand potential safety threats, the risks they could pose to your location, and the likelihood they could occur. In the case of thunderstorm winds, that means understanding how and why they occur, the particular risk to the area in which you're planning an outing, and, of course, checking the forecast.

Why does a thunderstorm produce such strong winds? Consider its size; an average thunderstorm is bigger than Mount Everest, which at 29,029 feet is no minor bump in the landscape. Some of the very biggest thunderstorms could practically hold two Mount Everests, stacked top to bottom. If a climber standing on the summit could throw a snowball all the way to the Rongbuk base camp, it would be flying at incredible

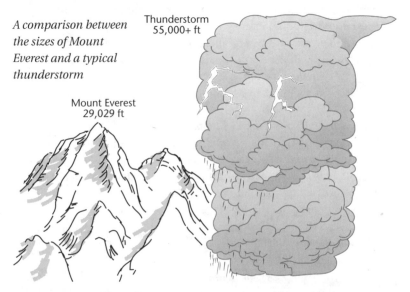

A comparison between the sizes of Mount Everest and a typical thunderstorm

Thunderstorm
55,000+ ft

Mount Everest
29,029 ft

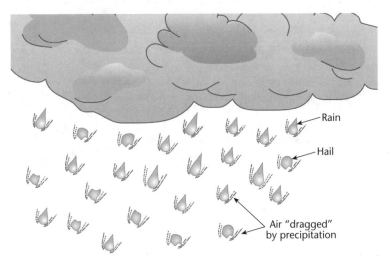

Rain

Hail

Air "dragged" by precipitation

How air is dragged by falling precipitation

speed by the time it hit the ground. Keep in mind that the altitude difference between the summit of Mount Everest and this base camp is approximately 12,000 feet. A hailstone thrown from a thunderstorm may have fallen two, three, or even four times that distance!

Also, a thunderstorm doesn't just drop one hailstone. During its mature and dissipating stages, it may dump more than a hundred million gallons of rain and hail. As those hailstones and raindrops fall, they move through air, which resists the falling precipitation. The hail and rain in turn pull some of the air along for the ride; that air is typically very cold—possibly well below zero.

That cold, dense air descends much faster than the surrounding air can warm it. The evaporation of rain cools it even more. The down-rushing air, or downdraft, continues to accelerate as it falls, hitting the ground with a resounding smack. This rain-cooled air plows ahead of the storm, often kicking up dust in a *gust front*. These gust fronts may span a dozen miles or more, and they are certainly strong enough to knock over trees, send tents flying, and swamp boats. They are typically marked by a long, horizontal tube-shaped *roll cloud*. If a cylinder-shaped cloud extends from the base of a thunderstorm, especially if it appears to be rotating, hit the deck! This *wall cloud* often precedes a tornado.

These signs have been known for decades. But in the 1970s, meteorologists studying unexplained air crashes found evidence of concentrated downdrafts. The ground damage where these extreme downdrafts

A thunderstorm wall cloud (photo courtesy of NOAA)

struck was far more severe than could be explained by an ordinary thunderstorm downdraft or gust front, but the pattern didn't suggest a tornado. Rather, it looked like a waterfall of air had hit the ground. Researcher Ted Fujita was intrigued when he flew over impact zones that showed a starburst pattern of downed and uprooted trees. He devised the term *downburst* to distinguish such events from their less lethal and destructive counterparts. These downbursts tend to have both sharp boundaries and a short lifetime. While maximum winds may reach 60 miles per hour within the downburst, winds outside of the impact zone may not reach even 10 miles per hour; from start to finish, the downburst may last only 3 minutes.

Dust and dirt stirred up by a descending microburst
(photo courtesy of NOAA)

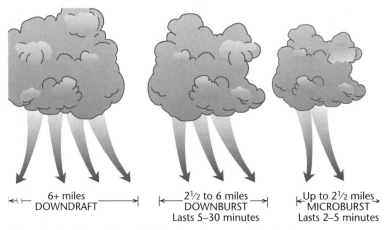

6+ miles	2½ to 6 miles	Up to 2½ miles
DOWNDRAFT	DOWNBURST	MICROBURST
	Lasts 5–30 minutes	Lasts 2–5 minutes

The relative sizes of downdrafts, downbursts, and microbursts

Fujita also discovered downbursts that occurred over extremely short distances, approximately 2.5 miles or less. He called these *microbursts.* Both downbursts and microbursts can plunge out of thunderstorms producing precipitation, or out of thunderheads in which the rainfall evaporates before it hits the ground. These dry thunderstorms are especially common in the arid parts of the western United States and northern Mexico. The evaporation of the falling rain cools the cascading air, strengthening the intensity of the downburst or microburst.

Meteorologists recognized that not all of the severe thunderstorm wind damage was brief and localized. Some of it came from organized lines of thunderstorm cells that tended to develop a bow shape on radar screens as they matured. Such displays came to be known as *bow echoes,* and the storms that generate them as *derechos (day-ray-chose),* from the Spanish word for "straight ahead." Derechos are essentially long-lived downbursts.

This was exactly the kind of storm that raced through North Dakota, northern Minnesota, and southern Ontario and Quebec on July 4, 1999. It was born far to the west the day before from a series of thunderstorms over southeastern Montana and western South Dakota that had merged the evening of July 3. The thunderstorm complex evolved into a derecho with its characteristic bow shape early on the morning of July 4, approximately 40 miles west of Fargo, North Dakota. Sweeping across northern Minnesota at speeds of up to 80 miles per hour, the derecho gained strength by the minute. It left several swaths of destruction; the worst was to the east of Ely in the Boundary Waters Canoe Area Wilderness—

exactly where Pete Esposito's scout group had been trapped. About 478,000 acres of forest were leveled in a swath 12 miles wide by 30 miles long. Uprooted trees, broken limbs, and crushed tree trunks, some stripped of their bark, were piled 15 to 20 feet high. Twenty campers required airlift evacuation to hospitals.

For a storm to qualify as a derecho, it has to create absolute meteorological mayhem, specifically, three different reports of hurricane-force winds, each separated by at least 40 miles, and a damage path of at least 250 miles. It's not unusual for derechos to spawn tornadoes. The July 4 derecho qualified easily. Although the derecho tends to be most common in Oklahoma and Kansas, it can and has been found anywhere from the Texas panhandle north into the Dakotas, and east through the Great Lakes all the way to the Appalachians.

Remember, you can anticipate the following about dangerous thunderstorm winds:

► They can occur beneath a thunderstorm whether rain is reaching the ground or evaporating aloft.
► They can occur ahead of the thunderstorm in gust fronts.
► They can spread out from beneath the thunderstorm.
► Wind speeds can easily reach or exceed hurricane force.
► They can last just seconds or persist much longer.

The other part of anticipating dangerous thunderstorm winds is checking the forecast, both before you leave home and, if possible, when you

Movement of the July 4, 1999 derecho through northern Minnesota

arrive at the trailhead or shoreline, and even during your trip. It's important to get your forecasts from agencies or sources familiar with your local area; forecasts issued by the National Weather Service come from such local offices, as do forecasts issued by qualified meteorologists working for local television or radio stations. Each of these sources also usually posts its forecasts on websites. Commercial forecast services working out of a single national office simply can't appreciate the local factors that can make a big difference. As mentioned in Chapter 5, it's important to check the forecast the day before you leave home, the day of the trip, and, if you have the opportunity, when you arrive at your starting point—typically from a park ranger. If NOAA Weather Radio broadcasts are available and transmit to your destination, by all means take a weather radio along and know the frequencies for your destination. Such radios have an alarm function that can save your life. If weather forecasts mention potential thunder showers, anticipate the possibility of dangerous thunderstorm winds. Don't think that it can't happen to you.

2. Assess

Assessing the risk of dangerous thunderstorm winds comes from looking at the sky and your surroundings on the ground or water.

First, consider the sky. It offers several clues to look for in the field:

- Warm, humid air: low visibility and unseasonably warm temperatures when coupled with high humidity are explicit danger signs.
- Clouds change from white to dark gray or black.
- Lightning flashes, falling hail, or the sound of thunder.
- Blowing dust.
- Wind-whipped trees or other vegetation.
- Sudden increase in wave height.
- A roll cloud in advance of a thunderstorm.
- A rotating wall cloud.

Next, check your surroundings. Some terrain features will enhance or reduce thunderstorm winds, as well as the threat of wind-borne debris.

- Are the trees around you uniform in size, or are there some much taller trees that stick up above the canopy?
- Are nearby trees healthy, or do they appear diseased or weakened by insects?
- Is your location downwind of a gap, pass, channel, or canyon?
- Is there a hill, bluff, or large boulder upwind?
- Do branches hang over your campsite?

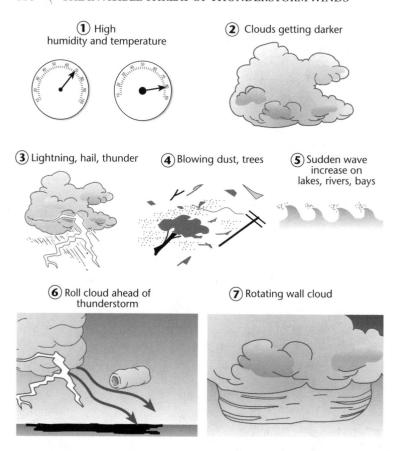

Warning signals of possible strong thunderstorm winds

Isolated trees or trees significantly taller than the surrounding stand will act as sails, catching more wind, and thus they are more likely to topple. Camp at a safe distance from them, as well as from trees that appear diseased or infested by insects. Caution signs include branches devoid of leaves, needles, or bark; trunks punctuated by woodpecker or flicker borings; and a coating of running sap or pitch. Such weakened trees will be among the first to drop in a strong wind. Narrow openings in the terrain, such as gaps, passes, channels, or canyons, focus and accelerate the wind. If thunderstorm winds (any winds for that matter) come blasting through such an opening, your tent (and possibly you) may go airborne! Avoid camping under overhanging branches if at all possible. Upwind bluffs, hills, or even large boulders or hedges upwind (to the west in most of North America, Europe, and Asia) can serve as windbreaks.

Features that may increase or decrease your exposure to damage or injury from strong thunderstorm winds

Once you've selected a campsite, erect your tent into the wind. Use solid tent stakes and guylines. Without guylines, even a moderately strong wind can snap tent poles. Experienced campers have found the best anchor comes from attaching guylines about one-third to one-half of the way up the tent.

Jim Brandenburg's decisions while photographing in the field are a perfect example of how sound assessment of the sky leads to positive actions. He had checked forecasts and knew thunderstorms were possible. He observed that the air was both unseasonably hot and very humid. Once Brandenburg noticed how dark the clouds were, he headed for shelter.

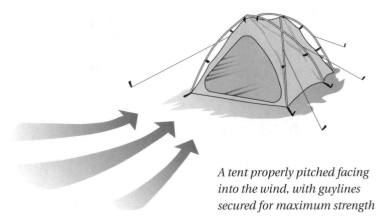

A tent properly pitched facing into the wind, with guylines secured for maximum strength

3. Act

Actions can either be reactive or preventive, positive or negative. Negative actions increase risk, while positive actions decrease it. The guidelines in the previous sections suggest positive, preventive actions to take *before* a storm hits. There are equally important, potentially life-saving actions to take *when* thunderstorm winds hit.

- ► Get out of your tent. A tent offers little protection and will prevent you from seeing falling trees.
- ► If you're in the woods, seek a stand of even-size trees. Avoid larger trees or trees that look dead or sick. Move toward a clearing or shoreline if possible.
- ► If you're in a clearing or along a shoreline, stay there; don't run into the woods.
- ► Crouch behind the side of a hill, bluff, or rock that's sheltered from the wind.
- ► If large trees are already downed to the ground, seek refuge beneath one.
- ► Crawl if the wind makes it too difficult to walk.
- ► Cover your head and face.

Pete Esposito's actions and those of his group during the Boundary Waters storm provide a perfect example of what to do. Esposito immediately got out of his tent, then directed the boys and their fathers to get out of their tents and away from the trees. He headed for an open clearing, in their case, the lakeshore. The fathers made a good choice, too; once they saw that the huge, fallen pine offered shelter, they ducked beneath it and held on.

① Get out of your tent

② Seek a stand of similar-sized trees

③ Stay near a clearing

④ Crouch behind a rock, bluff, or hill

⑤ Crawl if the wind makes it difficult to walk

⑥ Seek refuge beneath a fallen tree

⑦ Cover your head and face

Safe actions if strong thunderstorm winds threaten

4. Aid

When an injury occurs, the first step to take is to minimize the problem. If one injury has already occurred, don't add another by putting yourself at high risk while the storm is still raging. Before moving or attempting to help a victim, plan how you can minimize your exposure. A tree limb blowing at 60 miles per hour can kill. An unconscious or dead rescuer won't be of much use to someone needing help.

If possible, call for assistance.

Seeking assistance obviously depends upon your location and circumstances. If you're deep in the wilderness, you're on your own. If you're not alone and are within a couple miles of assistance, seek help. Are you carrying a cell phone? If so, try 911. However, remember that not all backcountry areas have 911 service and signals may not reach that far. Still, it's not a bad idea to carry the telephone number of the park headquarters or local fire or police agency. If you have a radio, use it to summon help. If it's not possible to communicate from your location and someone is injured, it's best to have someone remain with the injured person and send someone else for assistance. If your group is large enough, send two people. In all cases, make certain the storm is over before you move.

Signal for help.

Thunderstorm winds, such as those of the Boundary Waters storm, can leave you isolated and possibly unable to move. That will force you to catch the attention of searchers by signaling. If at all possible, move out into the open. Unless the fire danger dictates otherwise, build a smoky signal fire. Whistles, signaling mirrors, and flashlights can also be effective ways to get attention.

Carry a first-aid kit, know how to use it, and first treat those who appear to be dead.

Remember the ABCs of first aid: Check for an open *airway,* check to see whether the injured person is *breathing,* and then check for evidence of *circulation*—a pulse. Check for evidence of breathing and circulation for at least 20 to 30 seconds. If you can't detect breathing or circulation, begin CPR. (If you haven't completed CPR training or if it's been a while since you've practiced, sign up for and complete a new course now. It takes so little time to learn, and it can make a big difference.) If anyone is wet, treat for hypothermia. Put a protective layer between the victim and the ground to diminish the chance of hypothermia, and keep him or her warm by covering with any available clothing, blankets, or sleeping bags.

The scout group followed exactly the right steps in giving and seeking aid. They attempted to contact potential rescuers by radio. When that failed, they moved to a location with better visibility, built a smoky signal fire, and flapped every available bright object when a plane approached.

Set survival priorities.

To summarize, if immediate rescue isn't likely, set priorities:

- ► Keep a positive mental attitude—expect to survive.
- ► Administer first aid.
- ► Seek or build a shelter.
- ► Build a fire for warmth and signaling.
- ► Prepare rescue signals.
- ► Find water and purify if at all possible with boiling, filtering, drops, or tablets.
- ► Gather food. This ranks last in importance, but it can be a big morale builder.

Lightning and wind are just two of the four major thunderstorm dangers. The next chapter explores the third danger: flash flooding.

CHAPTER 7
THUNDERSTORMS AND FLASH FLOODS

Searchers emerged from Antelope Canyon, near the spot where the missing hikers disappeared. They were walking along the floor of the canyon, nearing the end of their hike, when the flood hit without warning . . . a roar of water shot through the narrow canyon walls . . . and swept away bodies like they were twigs. The main search effort is concentrated at the mouth of Antelope Canyon, where it enters Lake Powell. The flash flood dumped tons of mud and debris here and perhaps also the bodies of the missing hikers.

Reporter V. Reece Stein, KUTV News, Salt Lake City, Utah, August 13, 1997

The beauty of the night sky in the American Southwest's canyon country is breathtaking. The dry desert air reveals a rare brilliance and intensity. It seems as though the stars are almost touchable. That same clarity lends the frequent desert thunderstorms a startling sense of proximity: The lightning is more vivid and more threatening. There's no question that it's dangerous to be caught on a mesa or ridgeline in a thunderstorm, but perhaps the greatest danger from thunderstorms is in a place that paradoxically seems the safest—deep within the canyons.

In particular, slot canyons are so narrow it's possible to reach out and touch both walls at once. Looking up, only a narrow slit of sky is visible. That's part of what makes hiking into slot canyons so irresistible. Soft shades of tan, brown, ocher, and pink surround explorers within the canyon's softly undulating depths. It's easy to forget what produced those smooth curves: the powerful carving force of water. Not the slow trickle of water over eons, but the powerful, pulsing force of raging flash floods.

Cindy Purcell learned quickly the suddenness and power of flash floods. A district ranger for Zion National Park in southern Utah, she'd only been on the job one week when she joined the technical search and rescue team for a practice outing in the canyons. As they collected their gear and set out along the trail, Purcell felt a mix of eagerness and nerves.

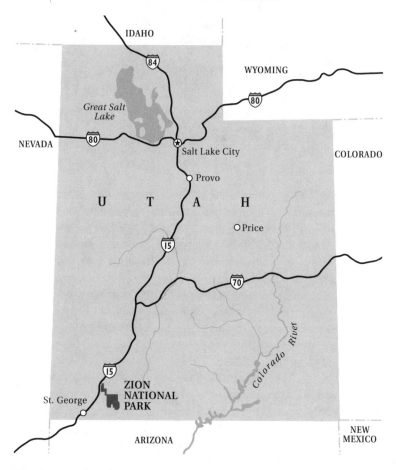

Zion National Park in Utah

She enjoyed the discipline of technical climbing and looked forward to using her skills to descend into these canyons. However, as they hiked along the west rim of the park toward Angels' Landing, she noticed the sky was already partly cloudy. The weather forecast was for a 60 percent chance of rain. Purcell had read the flash flood warnings issued to visitors and had reviewed the accident reports. This didn't seem a wise time to explore the canyons, but she was new and wanted to make a good impression. The other seven rangers were highly experienced. Purcell decided to stick with them.

As they pushed through brush and set up the ropes and anchors for the first descent into Behunin Canyon, Purcell's attention moved from her concerns to the tasks at hand. The group would be rappelling, or descending by sliding down a rope, about 200 feet to the first canyon floor, which would then descend lower in a series of steps.

Although rappelling looks to be fun and easy, it's statistically one of the most dangerous tasks in climbing. First, secure anchors had to be fixed along the canyon rim with backups for insurance; the ropes would then be led through the anchors and connected to the canyoneers' harnesses for the descent. Purcell was impressed by her colleagues' sure precision and attention to detail. After the always nerve-wracking initial descent over the lip of the canyon, she focused on maintaining a safe descent speed, keeping the ropes untangled, and on the beauty: small hanging gardens of wildflowers fed by seep springs, melodies from unseen songbirds, and then ancient silence in the depths. It's difficult not to be struck by a sense of sacredness in Zion's canyons.

The concerns about the rain forecast vanished as the group alternately hiked on soft sand and rappelled farther into the canyon, the sky becoming more remote with each passing minute. Subsequent events make it difficult to remember exactly when they noticed the small ribbon of sky was no longer blue but a dark gray. Her earlier sense of doubt welled into fear; a thunderstorm no longer was only a statistical possibility in a forecast: It was looming overhead. The group was in imminent danger of being caught in a flash flood. Purcell was no longer the only one concerned; risk has a way of focusing attention, and each canyoneer was now focused on getting out. There was one 300-foot rappel left, and it was the only way out of the slot. Anchors were being set just as the sky

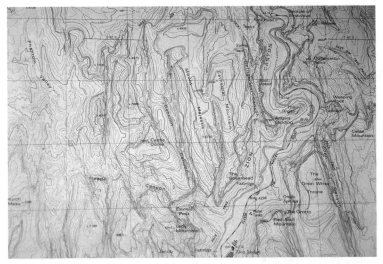

USGS map of the Behunin Canyon area in Zion National Park, Utah

opened up: first rain, then pounding hail, then a downpour. No one needed to be urged to descend swiftly because staying put would have been riskier. Purcell remembers looking to her left as she descended and noticing a waterfall. She may have been new to the park, but she realized it shouldn't be there. Two last canyoneers were on the rope, beginning their descent, as the waterfall broadened from a stream to a torrent, blasting beyond and down the rockface, seemingly swallowing the two men on the rope. They simply disappeared. Purcell was certain they had to be dead, flattened by the force of the water against the canyon walls. Miraculously, seconds later the two men reappeared, safe but soaked. Once on the ground, their ghostly pale faces said it all: "I almost died."

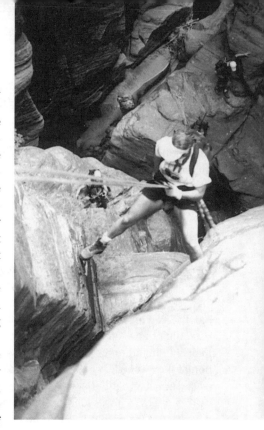

Canyoneer rapelling down slot canyon, Zion National Park (photo by Cindy Purcell)

Not everyone is so fortunate, and it's not only high-risk canyoneers who get caught. In 1998, two visiting hikers from California were swept to their deaths while hiking the slot canyon in Zion called the Narrows.

Rescue and recovery workers know all too well what to look for: first for signs of floating gear or equipment snagged on projections along walls, then for bodies washed ashore or floating in rivers. Since 1950, there have been twenty-two flash-flood fatalities in Utah. Flash floods kill regularly in other states, too. Eight hikers died in a single flash flood in northern Arizona's Antelope Canyon. Perhaps the most infamous flash flood occurred along Colorado's Big Thompson River on July 31, 1976. A thunderstorm developed during the early evening, dropping up to 12 inches of rain. The death toll hit 139, and not just in narrow stretches of the canyon. Some who died were caught in homes and even motels that were obliterated by the wall of water.

THE POWER OF WATER

Flash flooding poses a risk to any canyon in a thunderstorm, and you should always be alert before entering one. That risk multiplies with three factors in particular: canyon depth, width, and slope steepness.

As the illustration on page 123 indicates, the deeper the canyon, the greater the potential for water runoff to force a fast rise in water level. A wide valley will hold the same amount of water as a narrow one, but because there's so much room for the water to spread out, the depth will be shallow, perhaps ankle deep. The same amount of rain falling into a narrow canyon forces a rapid rise in the water level, perhaps neck deep or higher. You can see the same

Hikers in slot canyon, Zion National Park (photo by Cindy Purcell)

effect if you put a cup of water in a salad bowl as opposed to a tall but narrow flower base. As rain wets canyon walls, it is directed down and into a canyon. More water will drain off 500-foot canyon walls than off 50-foot walls. A narrow canyon, such as the Behunin slot canyon at Zion, will concentrate runoff into a smaller area, leading to bigger changes in stream level. Also, steeper slopes will support less vegetation, reducing the potential to absorb water and increasing potential runoff.

Keep in mind the power of a flash flood and that you can't swim in one because you'll get beaten to a pulp. Even a sudden flow of just 500 cubic feet per minute will hit with a force of more than 30,000 pounds! That's like being struck by a fully loaded semitrailer truck—if the impact alone doesn't kill you or knock you senseless, being flushed against the canyon walls or floating debris will. Your safety is your responsibility, and anytime you enter a narrow canyon, you're assuming a risk. Obtaining the current forecast is critical. Thus it is essential to follow the important safety guidelines established by the National Park Service. I present them in the context of the four As of Thunderstorm Safety:

1. Anticipate

► Check weather and flash flood forecasts before leaving home.
► Check for updated weather forecasts, flash flood forecasts, and canyon closures before leaving a trailhead.
► Remember that thunder showers, and therefore flash floods, tend to be most common from late June through August in the canyons of the U.S. West.

Waterfall generated by thunderstorm in slot canyon, Zion National Park (photo by Cindy Purcell)

Keep in mind that the percentage chance of precipitation doesn't suggest how intense the precipitation will be. A forecast calling for a 20 percent chance of showers or thunder showers doesn't mean they will be light showers. It means there's a 20 percent chance that measurable rain will fall at any given location, *but it doesn't have to be raining above you for a flash flood to occur.* Rain miles away may drain into a canyon and cause a flood.

Before entering a canyon, check with rangers, land management personnel, or whoever else might be knowledgeable about updated forecasts and closures. If a canyon is closed, it's for your safety. The canyon will always be there another day, but hikers ignoring such a closure may not.

2. Assess

Even the best prepared, most conscientious hiker or canyoneer may be caught by deteriorating conditions several days into a trip. That's why it's important to know the warning signs of a possible flash flood:

► Clouds building up or darkening above
► Sounds of thunder or flashes of lightning
► Sudden changes in water clarity from clear to muddy
► Sudden appearance of floating debris in water
► Rising water levels or stronger currents
► An increasing roar of water upcanyon
► Sudden appearance of waterfalls on canyon walls

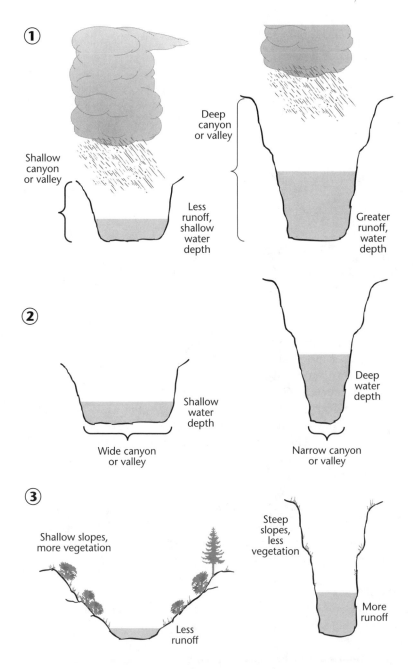

The effect of canyon shape and size on potential flash flooding

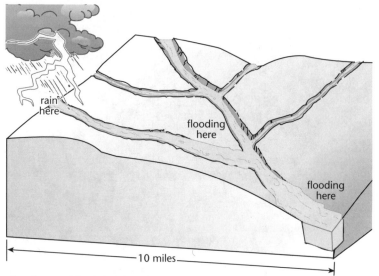

rain here

flooding here

flooding here

|← 10 miles →|

The threat of flash flooding from distant thunderstorms

3. Act

If you see or hear any of the signs pointing toward a flash flood, you don't have long to take the following actions:

► Seek higher ground immediately; even climbing a few feet may be the difference between life and death.
► If no higher ground is available, take shelter behind a rock jutting from the canyon wall. That may break some of the impact of the floodwaters.
► If possible, wedge yourself into a crack above water level.
► Remain on high ground until water levels drop and water clarity improves.

Typically, water levels drop within 24 hours of a flood; the possibility of an unexpectedly longer stay makes it especially important to carry the Ten Essentials (see below) on any hike, no matter how short. That's why you should always be prepared to aid yourself and/or others.

4. Aid

The possibility of being stranded, together with the potential for injury and hypothermia, are good reason to always carry the Ten Essentials:

The Ten Essentials

1. Extra clothing
2. Extra food and water (*Remember:* You can last much longer without

food than you can without water.)

3. Sunglasses and sunscreen
4. Knife
5. Firestarter
6. First-aid kit
7. Matches (in a waterproof container)
8. Flashlight or headlamp (with extra bulb and batteries)
9. Map
10. Compass

Signals of possible flash flooding

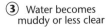

① Darkening sky

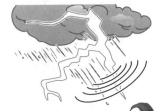

② Presence of thunder, lightning

③ Water becomes muddy or less clear

④ Floating debris appears

⑥ Sound of roaring water upcanyon

⑤ Water level rises or current increases

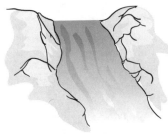

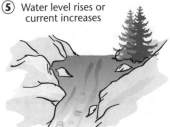

Keep in mind that even the most agile hiker can slip into the water, giving the important equipment listed above a thorough dunking. Consider carrying plastic trash bags and zip-type bags to waterproof your gear inside your pack. The possibility of a dunking in cool water is why hypothermia is a big risk in canyon country.

HYPOTHERMIA SIGNS AND TREATMENT

If you or a partner take a dunking or get soaked by rain and then chilled, be on the lookout for hypothermia. Following are the warning signs:

Complaints of feeling cold
Violent shivering
Stumbling, poor coordination, falling
Slurred speech
Irrational behavior

If you're unsure if it's hypothermia, have the person in question (including yourself, if you're feeling ill or odd) try to walk a straight line for 25 to 30 feet; if the result resembles a snake dance, treat for hypothermia.

First and foremost, exchange wet clothes for dry clothes and get the victim out of the elements and into a shelter.

Wrap the victim in a space blanket or a dry, prewarmed sleeping bag.
Sharing body warmth is an option.
Insulate from the ground.
Cover the head.
Feed warm drinks (nonalcoholic!) and sweets.
Evacuate as soon as possible and seek professional medical care.

A sleeping bag can be prewarmed by having someone who isn't chilled crawl into the bag first. Having that person share the bag with the hypothermia victim is an excellent method of rewarming. If the victim has a bad case of hypothermia, medical experts emphasize that it's important to handle him or her gently, as any jarring can trigger a fatal arrhythmia (an alteration of the rhythm or force of the heartbeat).

Lightning, damaging winds, and flash floods are three of the four dangers posed by thunderstorms in the backcountry. The next chapter explores the fourth: fires.

CHAPTER 8
FROM SKY FIRE TO WILDFIRE

It came in a rage and a crown to the top of the ridge . . . the fire stands on the ridge, roaring for hell to arrive as re-inforcement. While you are trying to peer through it to see the inferno on its way, suddenly somebody yells, "God, look behind! The son of a bitch has jumped the gulch!" One hundred and eighty degrees from where you have been looking for the inferno and halfway up the opposite ravine, small smoke is growing big where one of those burning cones or branches dropped out of the sky and trapped you with a fire in your rear. Then what do you do?

USFS 1919: The Ranger, the Cook, and a Hole in the Sky, Norman Maclean

Leavenworth, Washington, sits at the junction of the Icicle and Wenatchee Rivers, framed by the sheer Cascade Range to the west and rolling fruit orchards to the east. A popular destination for hikers, backpackers, rock climbers, whitewater kayakers, and others who simply want to drink in the scenery, it seems to have been transplanted from the Alps. In fact, when the town fell upon hard times, local merchants chose to adopt a Bavarian alpine theme in hopes it would attract tourists. Several decades of hard work later, that gamble paid off handsomely.

Bob and Kathryn Harrild, like many other residents, enjoyed visiting Leavenworth so much that they moved there in 1978 and bought a small bed and breakfast called Haus Rohrbach at the foot of Tumwater Mountain. They had seen many dry summers, and more than a few fires in the peaks and ridges surrounding their home. The Harrilds knew that lightning would typically bring spotter planes and then fire-fighting crews. The fires were always put out quickly.

It had been a dry year throughout 1994, and not just in Washington, but throughout the West. Hikers heading up the popular trails to the storied Enchantment Lakes were unnerved by the particularly crisp crunch of bone-dry pine needles underfoot. So were Forest Service fire management officials; they knew disaster could be just one bolt of lightning away.

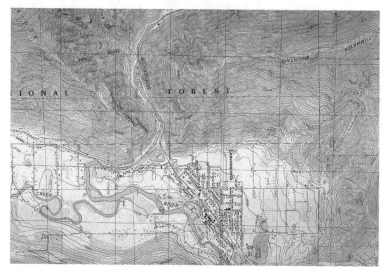

Leavenworth, Washington area. USGS map

In late July, fire-weather forecasters had warily watched as a tongue of hot, dry air surged north from the interior valley of California into Oregon. On July 24, this air mass brought thunderstorms but little rain. The next day, plumes of smoke dotted the Oregon Cascades. As the afternoon heat intensified on July 25, thunderstorms erupted anew, leap-frogging up the spine of the Cascades into Washington. The lightning strikes seemed endless. Forty separate fires were blazing the next day, the worst in Chelan County, uncomfortably close to Leavenworth.

These were not the fires that creep quietly underground, nor those that simply clear dead vegetation from the forest floor and leave the trees largely unscathed. Ample dry wood and needles allowed the lightning-triggered flames to quickly bolt up into the canopy of ponderosa pine and western larch, turning them into incandescent torches blazing at temperatures in excess of 1,800°F. Exploding pitch and water vapor within the trees rained burning embers in all directions. Ribbons of smoke quickly blossomed into brown clouds tinted with orange, reflecting flames below.

The Harrilds were enjoying a few quiet moments seated in lawn chairs in front of Haus Rohrbach. A thin banner of smoke drifted over-head. Both realized it came from a fire close to the fire camp. It'll be out soon, they thought. Forty-five minutes later, the thin banner had swelled into a dark mushroom of smoke, towering over the ridge. "Oh my God," thought Kathryn. "This may be trouble." Shortly afterward, her sister called from near the Icicle River. "The whole valley is black," she reported.

The Harrilds drove down to look. "It looked like wall-to-wall fire," Kathryn remembers, "filled with black smoke."

Authorities began closing roads down the Icicle, up the Tumwater. In short, just about every road into or out of town except for US 2 east. "We knew then we were all in big trouble," said Kathryn.

It wasn't long before hotshot fire crews rumbled up Ski Hill Drive to the Forest Service access road that wound up Tumwater Mountain behind Haus Rohrbach: crew bus after crew bus, Caterpillar tractors and dump trucks. Helicopters soon thundered overhead almost nonstop; the Harrilds volunteered the use of their field as a landing pad. The strategy was straightforward, but the execution was difficult: to create a buffer zone to halt the advancing fire, a barren swath in which there was nothing to burn. It was challenging work under the best conditions. Add the heat, altitude, and advancing flames, and it was exhausting. Smoke veiled the sky, the sun only a reddish glow. It was hard to breathe. When the Harrilds weren't providing refreshments to the crews, they were drawing water from their reservoir to wet the shrubs and trees surrounding their bed and breakfast, which in the long run might be unneeded, might be useless. All guests had long since left. For the Harrilds, what remained was nonstop tension, the recognition that sixteen years of work might soon go up in smoke. "We realized that even if we saved the buildings, our business might be ruined. Who would want to hike or snowshoe through forest fire rubble?" Bob wondered. Still, the couple couldn't sit still.

1994 Leavenworth fire (photo by Bob Harrild)

Rain was needed, but none came. The wind rose and shifted to the northwest, driving the blaze downslope toward Haus Rohrbach, down toward Leavenworth. The flames easily jumped the fire line the hotshots had labored hours to build. Crew buses full of exhausted firefighters raced down the mountain road, followed by the tractors and dump trucks. "I didn't know you could move a D-8 Cat that fast," said Bob. "The eyes of the hotshots, they were as big as saucers." It recalled the legendary response of a trainee taking a Forest Service examination: "What do you do when a fire crowns? Get out of the way, and pray like hell for rain." Hell came, but the rain didn't.

The hotshot crews were replaced by firefighters with tanker trucks. The attempt to contain this fire had failed; what remained was only the hope of saving the buildings. As the weak glow of daylight disappeared, one young firefighter knocked at the Harrilds' door. "Do you have any snakes around here?" he asked nervously. Bob, exhausted and discouraged as he was, suppressed a smile. Guests who came back year after year to hike, climb, ski, and enjoy the Harrilds' hospitality knew Bob's irrepressible humor was matched by a wicked sense of mischief. "Huh?" Bob responded, pretending uncertainty. The firefighter fidgeted and glanced around, perhaps convinced a hissing serpent was about to slither between his booted feet. He seemed reluctant to say the word, finally blurting out, "You know, rattlesnakes!" He was obviously from west of the mountains, which wasn't rattlesnake country. "Oh," Bob slowly nodded knowingly. "You mean our Leavenworth ground trout." With panic rising, the young man's voice quavered, "Do they come out at night?" Bob smiled, paused a second, then half chuckling, added, "Why don't you sleep inside?" That invitation was quickly accepted.

The Leavenworth ground trout remained at bay, the firefighters gained some much needed rest that night, conditions changed, and the fire was eventually halted short of Haus Rohrbach and the private homes on Ski Hill Drive. Ironically, Bob Harrild didn't get to see the flames halted, or watch the crews leave with the satisfaction that comes from success. He suffered a massive heart attack. When he returned later that summer after a multiple bypass operation, it was to an intact and still scenic Leavenworth. Incredibly, although 186,000 acres burned in Chelan County, no one died: not any of the hard-working firefighters or any backcountry hikers. Wildfires don't always have such a happy ending.

Of the forest fires in the western United States, 70 percent are set off by lightning strikes, as were many of the 1994 Chelan County fires. In a clinical sense, such fires can be an important part of maintaining an eco-system. Some trees, such as the lodgepole pine, will not release seeds from their cones until the heat of a fire loosens the gummy resin that binds them. It's this recognition that has transformed fire management policies from the traditional Smokey the Bear "Extinguish all fires" prac-tice toward the recognition that some fires can be beneficial, even serv-ing to prevent worse fires that might escalate from the accumulation of natural fuels over the years. Loud, exciting, frightening, and smoky, such fires even exhibit a certain beauty. But it's a beauty to contemplate from a distance—a considerable distance.

Wilderness and wildfire are inseparable; spend enough time in the wilderness and you'll probably encounter wildfire. Such an encounter will be awe-inspiring, and probably frightening, but it doesn't have to be dangerous or deadly. It does require, as wildland firefighters like to say, that you keep your wits about you.

1. Anticipate

Backpackers and other outdoorspeople can avoid most wildfire situa-tions by answering one question: How dry is my destination? The drier the vegetation, the greater the potential for wildfire. Some areas will be predictably dry at the same time each year; the Southwest in summer is just one example. Others will vary in dryness from year to year, with a particularly dry year from time to time. Anticipate the potential for wild-fire by checking reliable sources, such as the local U.S. Forest Service office and seasonal rainfall records from the local National Weather Ser-vice office. It's a simple and quick task.

Seasonal rainfall records can be found in the weather sections of most newspapers, as well as on websites of local offices of the National Weather Service. Scan headings and links for a reference to climate data, and then search for a comparison of rainfall. Monthly rainfall is helpful but may miss more important long-term dryness trends. Year-to-date or seasonal rainfall will be more helpful in detecting a potential problem. Rainfall 20 percent below normal warrants your attention; rainfall 40 percent or more below normal demands it.

Following is a partial excerpt from a daily climate summary for Yakima, Washington, that was issued by the National Weather Service office in Pendleton, Oregon. Note the precipitation for the year to date: 1.85 inches, which is almost exactly 40 percent below normal. That would be reason to be cautious!

CLIMATE REPORT
NATIONAL WEATHER SERVICE, PENDLETON OR
526 P.M. PDT THU APR 26 2001

....

... THE YAKIMA CLIMATE SUMMARY FOR 26 APRIL 2001
VALID TODAY AS OF 0500 P.M. LOCAL TIME

CLIMATE NORMAL PERIOD 1961 TO 1990
CLIMATE RECORD PERIOD 1909 TO 2001

WEATHER ITEM	OBSERVED VALUE	TIME (LST)	REC. VALUE	YR.	NORMAL VALUE	DEP. FROM NORMAL
TEMPERATURE						
TODAY						
MAXIMUM	82	324P.M.	87	1926	66	16
MINIMUM	53	1209A.M.	24	1948	38	15
AVERAGE	68				52	16
PRECIPITATION (INCHES)						
TODAY	0.09		0.44	1955	0.01	0.09
MO. TO DATE	0.50		MM	MM	0.45	0.05
SINCE 1 MAR	0.97		MM	MM	1.12	-0.15
SINCE 1 JAN	1.85		MM	MM	3.07	-1.22

Some local National Weather Service websites offer excellent fire weather summaries, packaging all the relevant weather and fire hazard information into a couple of pages. Sometimes even recent lightning strike locations are included.

The U.S. Forest Service offers extensive fire information on its websites, exploring past and current fires, as well as present and projected fire danger. Such information is as important as a current weather forecast if an outing is planned during the dry season or a drought.

2. Assess

Assessing the potential for lightning-caused (or human-caused) wildfires in the field should begin upon your arrival at the trailhead. Fire-danger signs will be posted at the entrances of most national parks and national forests. If the danger level is rated as high or extreme, your vigilance must be equally elevated. Check with rangers or other personnel for any area closures or recent lightning activity. Resist the temptation to ignore such closures.

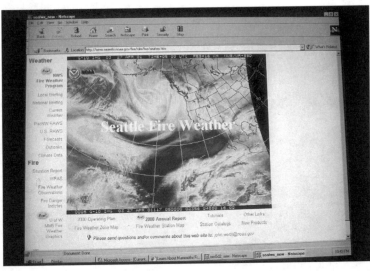

Seattle Forecast Office, National Weather Service website, fire information page (courtesy of NOAA)

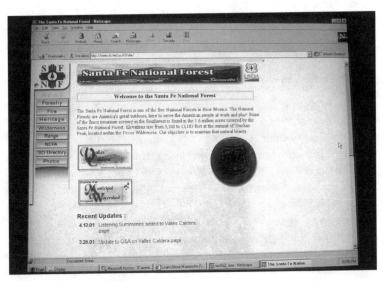

Santa Fe, New Mexico, National Forest website page (courtesy of U.S. Forest Service)

Example of Fire Danger Summary map (courtesy of U.S. Forest Service)

Once you've shouldered your pack, check for clues both in the sky and on the ground:

► Is the vegetation green and pliable or bone dry, brown, and crumbly?
► Are there piles of dead leaves or pine needles under trees that crunch underfoot?
► Are cumulus clouds forming or growing?
► Are the bases of the cumulus clouds low, that is, just above or near ridgelines, or are they high?

If the vegetation is dried and crumbly, it will make excellent fuel for fires. Growing cumulus clouds signal the potential for thunder showers. Low-based cumulo-nimbus can actually be helpful; they're more likely to produce needed rain. Lightning strikes can certainly occur, but the rain is likely to prevent such strikes from igniting fires. High-based cumulonimbus are a different matter. They're unlikely to produce rain, but very likely to produce lightning. If you observe thunderstorms forming with the bases substantially above ridgelines, be very alert, especially if they follow a string of sunny days. On clear days, ground temperatures may reach 160°F. The highest temperatures will be found on southwestern slopes during afternoon hours.

After checking for signs that might lead to a fire, look for signs that one might already be smoldering. One telltale sign might seem obvious: smoke. A *sleeper* is a fire that may remain hidden underground for days or a week or even longer, typically smoldering in dried roots, waiting for above-ground conditions to dry out enough for it to flare up, igniting vegetation above ground. One of the best clues that a sleeper may be smoldering underfoot is the presence on the ground of splintered pieces of tree or the shattered remains of a tree trunk. A lightning strike super-heats sap and water within a tree, forcing rapid expansion that literally blows a tree up from the inside out. In some cases, a tree may not heat up enough to explode, but it will typically show a spiral pattern of cracks down the tree trunk. Near such trees, odds are high there may be a sleeper fire underground.

Of course, there can be other, more obvious signs of fire, including the smell of smoke or clouds that are growing without a flat bottom. Flat-bottomed clouds are typically cumulus or cumulo-nimbus; those with round bottoms are generated by fire. You can be certain of fire if the cloud has a boiling appearance or is tinted with shades of orange or brown; the latter are reflections of flames beneath and smoke carried upward.

Signs of an Active Fire

- ► Splintered pieces of tree on the ground
- ► A shattered tree trunk, especially if it's blackened
- ► Smell of smoke
- ► Round-bottomed clouds that appear to "boil"
- ► Clouds tinted brown or orange

Key fire danger signs

(1) Is vegetation dry and crumbly?

(2) Are there crunchy piles of dead leaves or needles?

(3) Are cumulus clouds growing?

(4) Are cumulus bases high?

Splintered pieces of tree on the ground

Freshly shattered, and/or blackened tree trunk

Smell of smoke

Round-bottomed "boiling" clouds

Orange- or brown-tinted clouds

Key signs of possible or actual wildfire

3. Act

If smoke or actual flames are spotted, wildfire experts emphasize the safest action is to move downhill, and away. If you're downwind, the fire will tend to move toward you. Ridgelines are popular places to hike; travel is easier, views more spectacular, but they're the worst place to be in a wildfire. Because heat rises, flames tend to be drawn upslope and up valleys. Such upslope winds tend to be strongest on the south or southwestern slopes, which receive more direct sunlight during the warmer afternoon hours. The worst place to be is at the head of a fire, the leading edge of the flames as they advance. Fire can move much faster than any two-legged human.

While moving away, it's important to watch out for what are called *gravity hazards,* falling snags and rolling debris that are aflame. *Firewhirls* are another example of this threat. The heat generated by fires creates extreme instability in the air near the ground. The resulting violent cork-screw of wind can twist off trees larger than 3 feet in diameter, picking up and shooting out large embers, and setting off entirely new fires.

Even the coolest thinker will find it difficult to resist plunging over logs and rocks to escape a raging wildfire, but it's best to stay on the trail. Stress and haste can rob even the most agile of coordination. The possibility of injury is too great to risk bushwhacking your way out of a fire zone.

Experienced firefighters recommend looking for what they call safety areas: places that are unlikely to catch fire. Those would include rock-slides, wet meadows, lakes, ponds, rivers, or streams. When a fire isn't present, but conditions make a blaze possible, scout out such safety areas and the best evacuation routes.

To summarize, take the following actions when confronted by a fire:
- ► Move downslope and downwind of the fire.
- ► Stick to trails if at all possible.
- ► Watch out for gravity hazards: debris rolling downhill.
- ► Scout out safety areas and evacuation routes.

4. Aid

The best way to help others is to help yourself: Evacuate the fire zone promptly but carefully. Firefighters will have enough of a battle on their hands without having to search for and evacuate injured hikers. Warn others whom you may encounter, and then as soon as possible contact local authorities to report the fire.

How daytime heating generates upslope and upvalley winds

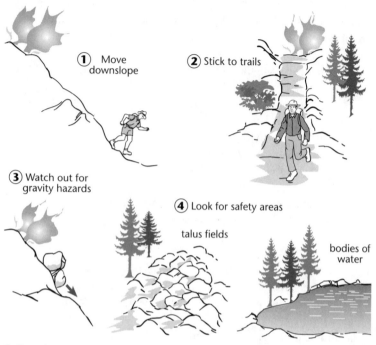

Safe actions to evade wildfires

Wildfires, like thunderstorm winds, flash floods, and lightning, demand respect. As Bob Harrild said of his experience with the Leavenworth fires, "I've been there. . . . I don't want to go there again." Neither do you. But with a little foresight, observation, and thought you don't have to. And you can still enjoy all the wonder of the wilderness—including thunderstorms.

CHAPTER 9
THUNDERSTORMS: THE AGELESS CHALLENGE

The odd thing about common sense is that it's not very common.
Voltaire

If a little knowledge is dangerous, where is the man who has so much as to be out of danger?
Thomas H. Huxley

Where thunderstorms are concerned, no one is truly ever out of danger, even when indoors. However, the point of this book is to foster both the confidence and sufficient knowledge you need to enjoy your time outdoors, pursuing your favorite activities. It may be tempting, from the comfort of an armchair, to wonder how some men and women who shared their outdoor experiences could make the errors they did. It's also tempting to believe those are errors you'd never make.

However, a lengthy mountain climb or hike, a tiring paddle across a lake, or a lengthy uphill ride on a mountain bike can leave us physically and mentally exhausted. Our judgment may no longer be operating at 100 percent, our observation powers no longer keen. After several days in the wilderness—or even after just a single day—the forecast we obtained before leaving home may have changed. It's not even necessary to venture very far outdoors to be exposed to dangers from thunderstorms. A car breakdown a few miles from town paired with one thunderstorm can spell trouble, as can a round of golf that has taken you several holes beyond the clubhouse when a squall line hits.

Technology is a powerful tool that can enhance our decisions and safety. Radar, satellites, automated weather observation stations, and computerized forecasting aids all make possible far better detection and forecasting of changes in the weather. Television, radio, the Internet, and other evolving media make it easier to be better informed and prepared. Each can help our weather judgment. None is a substitute for it.

Consider some of the stories told in this book: the Whittaker brothers on Mount Rainier, Jim Brandenburg and Pete Esposito in northern Minnesota, Cindy Purcell in Zion National Park, myself in the Canadian Rockies. What enabled each of us either to survive or to avoid a dangerous thunderstorm encounter wasn't technology as much as knowledge and judgment. Each of us was exposed to danger, and we all had to observe carefully and think our way to safety. Survival is the purpose of the four As of Thunderstorm Safety (anticipate, assess, act, and aid): tools that help us observe carefully and skillfully and think our way to safety. They're effective and easily remembered guidelines. The following paragraphs explore their value one more time:

1. Anticipate

Information and understanding provide the foundation for accurately anticipating potential trouble, such as weather information gathered before a trip as well as an understanding of thunderstorm behavior and dangers. You've read in this book about how to use technology to obtain the best information possible from a variety of sources to guide your planning decisions before you leave. You've also expanded your knowledge of what thunderstorms are, how they can develop, and the different dangers they can pose. The intent hasn't been to make you a meteorologist, but rather an informed weather consumer at home and a skilled weather observer in the field. Centuries, even millennia before the scientific method was developed, men and women who lived close to nature were careful observers of nature, and like prehistoric hunters, they ignored her warnings at their peril.

2. Assess

Assessment is a skill exercised in the field. It involves the blending of careful observation with knowledge, resulting in a decision that will maximize both your safety and enjoyment. Are clouds darkening and swelling upward? You know that can be a sign of a developing thunderstorm, particularly if a careful examination of forecasts before you left home led you to anticipate this possibility. Can you see lightning and hear thunder? Using the flash/bang principle can help you assess whether the storm is approaching your campsite. If you're deep within a canyon, blue sky is disappearing, and the river is changing color from a clear blue to a muddy brown, you know this can indicate an impending flash flood. Assessing your environment is like breathing: You should never stop. Though it might seem like work, it also heightens your appreciation of the outdoors.

3. Act

Anticipation based on understanding and preparation, careful assessment stemming from good observation, and a foundation of knowledge will be helpful only if followed by appropriate action. If you're high on a peak and you see storm clouds developing, you must act by getting lower. If lightning is approaching and no shelter is available, you know the proper action is to get away from metal objects, crouch in a low spot, and cover your ears. If you hear branches or trees falling from powerful thunderstorm winds, you recognize the need to seek shelter behind a large boulder or in a clearing away from trees. Appropriate action has to follow anticipation and careful assessment.

4. Aid

Even timely action can't always prevent injury or the need for assistance. It might be aid that you offer, or aid that you seek, for yourself or someone else. This, too, requires knowledge, which goes back to our first step: anticipation.

Experience cements knowledge in a way that no amount of study can. How-ever, few, if any, of the people who generously shared their experiences for this book would probably recommend that you learn thunderstorm safety the way they did. I know I wouldn't recommend flying into a thunderstorm, even a small one, to gain an appreciation of its power. I don't think Jim Brandenburg or Pete Esposito would suggest seeking out a severe thunderstorm to learn how to respond to life-threatening winds. Cindy Purcell certainly wouldn't advise rappelling into a slot canyon during a thunderstorm to practice evading flash floods, and it's certain that Bob Grant and the Whittakers wouldn't advise climbing a peak to see whether you really understand how to avoid being struck by lightning. Their experiences provide you with the opportunity to put yourself in their shoes, to better anticipate what led to their hair-raising adventures, to see how they assessed the dangers, why they acted the way they did, and why their actions helped. Their experiences can aid you. In fact, you're probably already safer because of the knowledge you've gained from their experiences.

Confronted by a raging thunderstorm on an exposed mountain peak or a windswept lake, we moderns know better than to believe it's an attack by a troll, devil, or giant (though our subconscious may have some doubts). It's natural to feel fear in the face of such immense power because, despite our modern urge to manage just about everything, thunderstorms are unmanageable. The solution isn't to stay indoors whenever a cloud appears, though. The challenge is to manage ourselves wisely. See you outside.

APPENDIX

THUNDERSTORM SAFETY FIELD REFERENCE GUIDE

"I never believed that I could be in danger on a golf course—until I was struck by lightning on one last year. What I learned that spring day is that lightning is an underrated killer that fries minds and turns bodies into charred shells.

"...At forty-nine I am learning basic motor skills—to eat, shave, dress, walk down a hall without bumping into walls. I can't toss my little girl into the air.

"...Perhaps it is only natural that the press concentrates on dangers that threaten many people at once ... deaths and injuries from lightning are isolated and far-flung—easy to overlook or ignore. Unless, of course, you have been a victim."

Michael Utley, Lightning Victim
The New York Times Editorial/Op-Ed; August 27, 2001

It's the purpose of this book to reduce the number of casualties caused by thunderstorms; whether they're caused by lightning, winds, flash floods or wildfires. The previous chapters have built the foundation of thunderstorm knowledge. But now as you prepare to head outdoors, or are outdoors, you may wonder "Where were those guidelines on thunderstorm winds?" or "Where can I find the advice on lightning safety?" That's the objective of this appendix—to offer a quick reference guide to questions you might ask or should ask, both before you leave home or once you're outside.

The key is to remember the four As of Thunderstorm Safety: Anticipate, Assess, Act, and Aid. Blame it on this author's background as a flight instructor, but I've found checklists to be a handy tool to guide your thinking through stressful situations, and to guide you to safety. That's the spirit with which they're offered here.

ANTICIPATE (Or, questions to ask before leaving home.)

Anticipating potential thunderstorm danger begins with gathering information.

Question: What's the weather outlook?
Question: Are there any watches or warnings posted? What exactly do they mean?

Information Type	Source	Availability
Severe weather watches, warnings	National Weather Service	NOAA Weather Radio, TV and radio news, websites
Zone and state forecasts	National Weather Service, broadcast meteorologists	NOAA Weather Radio, TV and radio news, websites, newspapers
Extended outlook	National Weather Service, broadcast meteorologists	NOAA Weather Radio, TV and radio news, websites, newspapers
Satellite photos	National Weather Service	TV news, websites, newspapers
Weather radar	National Weather Service, broadcast meteorologists	TV news, websites
Weather observations	National Weather Service, private observers	NOAA Weather Radio, TV and radio news, websites
Private observations	State patrol, sheriff and police departments, state and national park rangers	Telephone or personal visit

Severe Thunderstorm Watch: Conditions are favorable in the watch area for thunderstorms to produce wind gusts to 58 mph or greater, hail 3/4-inch or larger, or tornadoes. None have actually been spotted in the watch area. Such watches are typically issued for four to six hours at a time, and for a number of counties.

Severe Thunderstorm Warning: A severe thunderstorm has been detected by radar, or by a trained spotter, or is imminent. Take cover immediately.

Tornado Watch: Tornadoes are possible in the watch area. Remain alert for approaching storms.

Tornado Warning: A tornado has been seen or is indicated by weather radar. Move to a place of safety immediately.

Flash Flood Watch: Flash floods are possible in the watch area. Remain alert; be prepared to move to a safer location.

Flash Flood Warning: Immediately take action to save yourself. You may only have seconds to act.

Question: Are any fronts approaching?
- Thunderstorms occasionally form along warm fronts and stationary fronts.
- Thunderstorms frequently form along cold or occluded fronts.
- Thunderstorms frequently form in the warm air between warm and cold fronts.
- Squall lines typically form along or ahead of a cold front.
- One squall line can form another squall line ahead of it.
- Expect strong gusty winds, hail, lightning, and possibly tornadoes.
- Widespread rain is likely even after a squall line dies or moves past.
- Strong winds can occur after a squall line moves past.
- Allow at least a half hour after squall line passage before venturing outdoors.

Question: Has a cold front just moved through?
If an upper trough is forecast to follow a cold front, assume thunderstorms may develop, particularly along the west slopes of mountains. Such thunderstorms are most common along the coastal ranges of the western United States and Canada.

Question: Am I headed for or near a coast?
- Sea breezes are strongest when other weather systems are absent and can produce thunderstorms, especially during the summer.
- Disturbances producing significant winds or clouds can prevent sea breezes from developing.

- Sea breezes typically develop during the late morning hours and peak during the afternoon.
- Sea breeze thunderstorms usually die out as the flow reverses late in the day, moving from land toward water.
- Particularly strong sea breeze thunderstorms are found over peninsulas.

Question: Am I headed for the mountains?
- Mountain thunderstorms are most frequent during the afternoon, particularly during the summer.
- Mountain thunderstorms are most frequent along the windward slopes, especially if cooler air has moved in aloft and sun is warming the slopes.
- Mountain thunderstorms may form downwind of smaller ranges or isolated peaks in a convergence zone.

Question: Am I headed for a canyon, valley, river- or streambed?
- Check flash flood forecasts before leaving home.
- Check for updated weather forecasts, flash flood forecasts, and canyon closures before leaving the trailhead.
- Thundershowers, and therefore flash floods, tend to be most common from late June through August.

Question: Has it been dry at my intended destination?
- Check for fire danger and trail or campground closures.

Question: What safety equipment should I take with me?
> **Ten Essentials**
> Extra Clothing
> Extra Food and Water
> Sunglasses and Sunscreen
> Knife
> Firestarter
> First Aid Kit
> Matches (in a waterproof container)
> Flashlight or Headlamp (with extra bulb and batteries)
> Map
> Compass
> And remember to let others know where you're going and when you

expect to return!

ASSESS (Or, questions to ask while outdoors.)

Question: Do the clouds I'm seeing suggest a change in the weather?

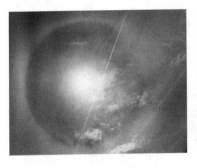

Halo, commonly seen 24–48 hours ahead of precipitation

Lenticular cloud, wavelike clouds over mountains often suggesting approaching precipitation

Cirrus clouds, high clouds often seen before the arrival of a warm front

Cirrostratus clouds, high clouds often seen before the arrival of a warm front

Altostratus clouds, mid-level clouds often seen after cirrus clouds and before the lower stratus clouds when a warm front is approaching

Stratus clouds, flat, layered clouds often seen with the approach of a warm front and precipitation, or the arrival of ocean air

Cumulus, lower clouds that mark unstable air. With continued growth, these often indicate the potential for thunder or rain showers later in the day.

Altocumulus, mid-level cumulus clouds marking unstable air that often indicate the potential for thunder or rain showers later in the day

Nimbostratus, stratus clouds producing widespread precipitation and often lowered visibility

Cumulonimbus. Cumulus clouds producing rain, snow or thunder, lightning and hail

Stratocumulus, lumpy, layered clouds that can produce showers

Question: What thunderstorm danger signals should I look for?

► Warm, humid air: Low visibility and unseasonably warm temperatures when coupled with high humidity are particularly danger signs.

► Clouds change from white to dark gray or black.

► Lightning flashes, falling hail, or the sound of thunder.

► Strongly blowing dust, trees, or vegetation together with dark clouds.

► Sudden increase in wave height together with dark clouds.

Question: I see lightning; how much am I at risk?

You are at greatest risk if:

► You are in the open.

► You are near or on isolated, tall objects.

► You are on or near water.

► You are near, wearing, or holding metal objects.

► You are feeling a tingling sensation or hearing a buzzing noise.

If any of the statements above are true, use the Flash/Bang Principle: Start timing at the lightning flash, stop timing at the thunder, divide by five to determine the storm's distance. Continue checking the storm's location.

Question: What signs might indicate a tornado?

► A rotating wall cloud beneath a thunderstorm

► Dark, sometimes greenish sky

► Large hail

► Loud roar; can sound like a jet airplane or freight train

► Dust or debris kicked up on the ground

► Tornadoes may develop in areas where severe thunderstorm watches or warnings are posted. But stay alert if any of the above clues are present, even if a tornado watch or warning hasn't been issued. Remember that hills, trees, clouds, or rain can hide tornadoes.

Question: I am in or near a wooded area; what factors could indicate potential hazards from thunderstorm winds?

► Are the trees around you uniform in size, or are there some much taller trees that stick up above the canopy?

► Are nearby trees healthy, or do they appear diseased or weakened by insects?

► Is your location downwind of a gap, pass, channel, or canyon? Winds can accelerate moving through such gaps.

► Is there a hill, bluff, or large boulder upwind? That could offer protection from winds.

► Are there branches overhanging your campsite? Thunderstorm winds could drop those on you. Choose a different spot.

Question: I'm in or about to enter a canyon, stream, or river valley. What signs could indicate a potential for flash flooding?
► Clouds building up or darkening above
► Sounds of thunder or flashes of lightning
► Sudden changes in water clarity from clear to muddy
► Sudden appearance of floating debris in water
► Rising water levels or stronger currents
► An increasing roar of water up-canyon
► Sudden appearance of waterfalls on canyon walls

Question: It's been very dry and thunderstorms are expected. What clues might indicate a potential for wildfires?
► If the vegetation is green and pliable or bone dry, brown, and crumbly.
► If there are piles of dead leaves or pine needles under trees that crunch underfoot.
► If cumulus clouds are forming or growing, a thunderstorm might soon develop.
► If the base of the cumulus clouds are high and develop into thunderstorms, they are more likely to produce lightning than rain. Low based cumulus clouds—just above or near ridgelines—are more likely to produce rain.

Question: It's been very dry and there have been lightning strikes recently. What might indicate a potential wildfire is already smoldering?
► Splintered pieces of tree on the ground, especially if it's blackened
► A shattered tree trunk, especially if it's blackened
► Smell of smoke
► Round-bottomed clouds that appear to "boil"
► Clouds tinted brown or orange

ACT (Or, important safety actions)
I see lightning. What should I do?
► Drop anything made of metal or graphite and move away from it.
► Move off a pinnacle, peak, ridgeline or hilltop.
► If you're in the water, get out immediately.
► If a vehicle or metal shelter is available, get inside. The metal exterior will shield you. Do not touch any metal handles during the storm.

- Do not use a telephone.
- Move away from isolated or tall trees. If in a wooded area, seek an area of lower trees of similar heights.
- If in an area of undulating hills, get to a low area.
- If caught in the open, crouch down, remaining on your feet and cover your ears. Do not lie down.
- If in a group of people, spread out.
- Use the Flash/Bang principle to determine storm movement. Begin timing at the lightning, stop at the thunder, divide by five to determine your distance from the storm in miles. Once the storm passes, wait until you can no longer hear thunder before leaving shelter.

Question: A thunderstorm is approaching, it's blowing hard, and I'm near trees. What should I do?
- Get out of your tent if you're in one. A tent offers little protection, and will prevent you from seeing falling trees.
- If you're in the woods, seek a stand of evenly sized trees. Avoid larger trees or trees that look dead or sick. Move toward a clearing or shoreline if possible.
- If you're in a clearing or along a shoreline, stay there; don't run into the woods.
- Crouch behind the leeward side of a hill, bluff or rock.
- If large trees are already down on the ground, seek refuge beneath or next to one.
- Crawl if the wind makes it too difficult to walk.
- Cover your head and face.

Question: It's raining and I'm in a canyon (or in a narrow stream or river valley). What should I do to protect myself from a flash flood?
- Seek higher ground immediately; even climbing a few feet may be the difference between life and death.
- If no higher ground is available, take shelter behind a rock jutting from the canyon wall. That may break some of the impact of the floodwaters.
- If possible, wedge yourself into a crack above water level.
- Remain on high ground until water levels drop and water clarity improves.

Question: There's a wildfire and I'm outside. What should I do?
- Move downslope and downwind of the fire.

- Stick to trails if at all possible.
- Watch out for gravity hazards—debris rolling downhill.
- Look for safety areas: rocky or other areas barren of burnable vegetation, or areas of water.

AID (Or, how can I help myself or others safely?)

Question: A companion has been struck by lightning. What can/should I do?

- First, cause no more casualties—do not expose yourself to lightning.
- Recognize the victim can't hurt you; you can't be electrocuted by touching someone who has been struck by lightning.
- If possible, send for assistance.
- Seek to first treat those who appear dead.
- Move the victim if lightning is still a threat, and if you can do so without endangering yourself.
- Perform CPR.

Question: Someone has been soaked by a flashflood or sudden immersion in water. What are the signs of hypothermia?

- Complaints of feeling cold
- Violent shivering
- Stumbling, poor coordination, falling
- Slurred speech
- Irrational behavior

Question: If I suspect hypothermia, what can I do to help?

- First and foremost, exchange wet clothes for dry clothes, and get the victim out of the elements and into shelter.
- Wrap in a space blanket or dry, pre-warmed sleeping bag.
- Shared body warmth is another option.
- Insulate the person from bare ground.
- Cover the person's head.
- Give the person warm drinks and sweets. Do not give the person alcoholic drinks.
- Evacuate the person as soon as possible and seek professional medical care.

Question: We're trapped, either because of downed debris, a disabled vehicle, or an injury. What should we do?

- If immediate rescue isn't likely, set priorities.
- Keep a positive mental attitude—expect to survive.

- ► Perform first aid.
- ► Seek or build shelter.
- ► Build a fire for warmth and signaling.
- ► Prepare rescue signals.
- ► Find water and purify it if at all possible through boiling, filtering, drops, or tablets.
- ► Gather food. This ranks last in importance, but can be a big morale-builder.

BIBLIOGRAPHY

CHAPTER 1

Beckey, Fred, *Cascade Alpine Guide 1: Columbia River to Stevens Pass.* Seattle: The Mountaineers Books, 2000.

The Seattle Daily Times

The Seattle Post-Intelligencer

CHAPTER 2

Beard, Mary, John North, and Simon Price, *Religions of Rome.* Cambridge, England: Cambridge University Press, 1998.

Bernbaum, Edwin, *Sacred Mountains of the World.* San Francisco: Sierra Club Books, 1990.

Bonvillain, Nancy, *Native American Religion.* New York: Chelsea House Publishers, 1996.

Burkert, Walter, *Greek Religions.* Cambridge, England: Cambridge University Press, 1985.

Clark, Ella, *Indian Legends of the Pacific Northwest.* Berkeley: University of California Press, 1953.

Ebrey, Patricia Buckley and Peter N. Gregory, eds, *Religion and Society in T'ang and Sung China.* Honolulu: University of Hawaii Press, 1993.

Mails, Thomas E., *Fools Crow.* New York: Doubleday and Co., 1979.

Pielou, E. C., *After the Ice Age: The Return of Life to Glaciated North America.* Chicago: University of Chicago Press, 1991.

Radin, Paul, *Primitive Religion.* New York: Dover Publications, 1957.

Ritzenthaler, Robert E. and Pat, *The Woodland Indians of the Western Great Lakes.* Milwaukee, Wisconsin: Milwaukee Public Museum, 1983.

CHAPTERS 3, 4, 5, 6, 9

Caracena, Fernando, Ronald Holle, and Charles A. Doswell III, *Microbursts: A Handbook for Visual Identification.* Boulder, Colorado: U.S. Department of Commerce/National Severe Storms Laboratory, 1990.

Dolan, Edward F., *The Old Farmer's Almanac Book of Weather Lore.* Dublin, New Hampshire: Yankee Books, 1988.

Houze, Robert Jr., *Cloud Dynamics.* San Diego: Academic Press, 1993.

Huschke, Ralph, ed., *Glossary of Meteorology.* Boston: American Meteorological Society, 1959.

Kotsch, William J., *Weather for the Mariner.* Annapolis, Maryland: Naval
Institute Press, 1983.

Lockhart, Gary, *The Weather Companion.* New York: John Wiley &
Sons, 1988.

Observer's Handbook. London: Her Majesty's Stationery Office, 1982.

Parke, Peter S., *Satellite Interpretation for Forecasters.* Temple Hills,
Maryland: National Weather Association, 1986.

Ray, Peter S., ed., *Mesoscale Meteorology and Forecasting.* Boston:
American Meteorological Society, 1986.

Renner, Jeff, *Northwest Mountain Weather.* Seattle: The Mountaineers
Books, 1992.

————, *Northwest Marine Weather.* Seattle: The Mountaineers
Books, 1993.

Thunderstorms and Lightning: A Preparedness Guide. Washington, D.C.:
U.S. Department of Commerce, 1994.

Williams, Jack, *The Weather Book.* New York: Vintage Books, 1997.

CHAPTER 7

Steele, Peter M.D., *Backcountry Medical Guide.* Seattle: The Mountaineers Books, 1999.

Weiss, Hal, *Secrets of Warmth.* Seattle: The Mountaineers Books, 1992.

CHAPTER 8

Schroeder, Mark J. and Charles Buck, *Fire Weather.* Washington, D.C.:
U.S. Department of Agriculture, 1977.

INDEX

A
ABCs of first aid, 93, 114
Aborigines, 28
air masses, 56, 58, 59

B
barometer, 58, 83
Boundary Waters Canoe Area
    Wilderness, 22, 95, 96, 97, 98,
    99, 107
bow echoes, 67, 68, 107
Brandenburg, Jim, 95, 96, 98, 99,
    111, 141
Brikoff, Paul, 16, 17, 18, 19, 21

C
Campbell, Joseph, 27
Chelan County, 23
Christensen, A.B., 20
cloud types
    altocumulus, 64
    altostratus, 63
    cirrostratus, 63
    cirrus, 63
    cumulonimbus, 64
    cumulus, 64
    fair weather Cumulus, 43, 45, 46
    halo, 63
    lenticular, 63
    nimbostratus, 64
    roll, 105
    stratocumulus, 64
    stratus, 60, 63
    wall, 105
condensation, 42
convection, 41, 42

D
Daiber, Ome, 20
deposition, 45
derecho, 68, 107, 108

dew point, 42, 43, 45, 83
downburst, 106, 107
downdrafts, 105, 106, 107

E
electrical potential, 47, 49
Esposito, Pete, 22, 98, 99, 100, 101,
    102, 103, 107, 112, 141

F
firewheels, 136
flash flood warning, 78
flash flood watch, 78
Flash to Bang Principle, 85
fronts, 56, 58, 59, 60, 61, 62
Fujita, Theodore, 106, 107

G
Grant, Bob, 16, 17, 18, 19, 20, 21,
    141
gravity hazards, 136

H
hailstone, 46, 48
Harrild, Bob and Kathryn, 127, 128,
    129, 130, 138
hypothermia, 94, 126

I
ice nuclei, 44, 45
ice pellets, 46
instability, 58

J
Jupiter, 30

L
Leavenworth, Washington, 127,
    128, 129, 130
lifting condensation level, 44
lightning, 47, 48, 49, 50, 51, 52, 74

lightning types
    ball, 74
    heat, 74
    red elves, 74
    red sprites, 74
    rocket, 74
    St. Elmo's Fire, 74
    sheet, 74
lightning man, 28

M
mastodon, 25
mesoscale convective complex, 68, 69, 70
mesoscale convective systems, 62
microburst, 106, 107
Moses, 30, 31
Mountaineers, Seattle, 20
Mount Stuart, 15

N
National Weather Service, 76, 77, 78, 79, 80, 99, 101, 131, 132, 133, 144

O
orographic effects, 55, 56, 58

P
Paleo-Indians, 26
Pleistocene, 28
pressure, high and low, 58, 59
Purcell, Cindy, 23, 117, 118, 119, 120, 141

R
rainbow serpent, 28
rain bands, 60
relative humidity, 43, 44, 83
Rodes, Dusty, 16

S
severe thunderstorm warning, 78
severe thunderstorm watch, 78
Shimon, Ed, 96, 97, 99, 101
sleeper fire, 135
squall lines, 62, 65, 66

stepped leader, 49, 51
streamer, 49, 51
supercooled droplets, 46
survival priorities, 115

T
Ten Essentials, 124, 125, 146
thermal, 43
thunderstorms
    air mass, 41, 54
    convergence, 56
    developing stage, 49
    dissipating stage, 52
    dryline, 66, 67
    gust front, 68, 105, 106
    mature stage, 49
    mountain, 55, 56
    postfrontal, 70, 71
    sea breeze, 56, 57. 58
    supercell, 68, 69, 70
    systems, 62
tornadoes, 72, 73
tornado warning, 78
tornado watch, 78
Tropopause, 46
Trott, Otto, 20

U
upper troughs, 70, 71
U.S. Forest Service, 127, 129, 130, 131, 132, 133

W
water vapor, 42, 43, 44
Weather Radio, NOAA, 77, 99, 109, 144
Whittaker, Jim and Lou, 39, 141
wind shear, 65, 68
Wisconsin, 25

Z
Zeus, 29, 30
Zion National Park, 23, 117, 118, 119, 120, 121

ABOUT THE AUTHOR

Jeff Renner is well known in the northwest as KING TV's chief meteorologist. An award-winning weather forecaster and science writer, he's written *Northwest Mountain Weather* and *Northwest Marine Weather* and is a contributing author to *Mountaineering: The Freedom of the Hills* all published by The Mountaineers Books. Jeff has spent a lifetime dealing with thunderstorms on the ground as a forecaster, skier, climber, and hiker, and in the air as a commercial pilot and flight instructor.

THE MOUNTAINEERS, founded in 1906, is a nonprofit outdoor activity and conservation club, whose mission is "to explore, study, preserve, and enjoy the natural beauty of the outdoors. . . ." Based in Seattle, Washington, the club is now the third-largest such organization in the United States, with 15,000 members and five branches throughout Washington State.

The Mountaineers sponsors both classes and year-round outdoor activities in the Pacific Northwest, which include hiking, mountain climbing, ski-touring, snowshoeing, bicycling, camping, kayaking and canoeing, nature study, sailing, and adventure travel. The club's conservation division supports environmental causes through educational activities, sponsoring legislation, and presenting informational programs. All club activities are led by skilled, experienced volunteers, who are dedicated to promoting safe and responsible enjoyment and preservation of the outdoors.

If you would like to participate in these organized outdoor activities or the club's programs, consider a membership in The Mountaineers. For information and an application, write or call The Mountaineers, Club Headquarters, 300 Third Avenue West, Seattle, WA 98119; 206-284-6310.

The Mountaineers Books, an active, nonprofit publishing program of the club, produces guidebooks, instructional texts, historical works, natural history guides, and works on environmental conservation. All books produced by The Mountaineers Books fulfill the club's mission.

Send or call for our catalog of more than 500 outdoor titles:

The Mountaineers Books
1001 SW Klickitat Way, Suite 201
Seattle, WA 98134
800-553-4453
mbooks@mountaineersbooks.org
www.mountaineersbooks.org

The Mountaineers Books is proud to be a corporate sponsor of Leave No Trace, whose mission is to promote and inspire responsible outdoor recreation through education, research, and partnerships. The Leave No Trace program is focused specifically on human-powered (nonmotorized) recreation.

Leave No Trace strives to educate visitors about the nature of their recreational impacts, as well as offer techniques to prevent and minimize such impacts. Leave No Trace is best understood as an educational and ethical program, not as a set of rules and regulations.

For more information, visit *www.LNT.org*, or call 800-332-4100.